THE HOMEMADE SAUSAGE COOKBOOK

Bertie Mayone Selinger
and
Bernadine Sellers Rechner

Contemporary Books, Inc.
Chicago

831338
9.95

Library of Congress Cataloging in Publication Data

Selinger, Bertie M. (Bertie Mayone)
  The homemade sausage cookbook.

  Includes index.
  1. Cookery (Sausages)   I. Rechner, Bernadine S.
(Bernadine Sellers)   II. Title.
TX749.S38   1982   641.6'6   82-45416
ISBN 0-8092-5864-1

Material quoted on pages 1 and 2 is from Homer, *The Odyssey*, translated by Robert Fitzgerald. Copyright © 1961 by Robert Fitzgerald. Reprinted by permission of Doubleday & Company, Inc.

Illustrations by Edward W. Rechner and Joel Rak

Photographs by Bernadine M. Rechner

Published by Contemporary Books, Inc.
180 North Michigan Avenue, Chicago, Illinois 60601
Manufactured in the United States of America
Library of Congress Catalog Card Number: 82-45416
International Standard Book Number: 0-8092-5864-1

Published simultaneously in Canada by
Beaverbooks, Ltd.
150 Lesmill Road
Don Mills, Ontario M3B 2T5
Canada

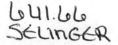

To my husband Paul, who encourages my growth by his love, gentleness, and patience.

To our daughters Olivia, Marilyn, and Martha for their encouragement and support. And to our retarded son Paul, Jr., whose presence in my life developed caring.

Bertie Mayone Selinger

For Ed and our kids—Carolyn, Kevin, and John—who keep the faith.

Bernadine Sellers Rechner

Contents

Introduction

Who cooks who does not share with family, friends, or associates, either daily or on special occasions? Cooking *is* loving. It is social sharing and it is nutritionally necessary.

The Homemade Sausage Cookbook was conceived out of need, the need to bring the art of making nutritionally superior, better tasting, less expensive sausage back into the home, where it originated thousands of years before the birth of Christ.

Homemade sausage is a completely edible, easy-to-make product. But sausage making has been left in the hands of the big producers for too long. With commercial sausage containing fat levels of up to 50 percent, with more salt in sausage than anyone needs, and with chemicals added which may be downright dangerous, it is time to renew the art of sausage making in our own kitchens.

The popularity of sausage continues to grow, yet few books are available which explain how—with ordinary kitchen equipment, a little meat, a smidgeon of fat, and a dime's worth of spices— you too can make Italian, Polish, and breakfast sausages plus a variety of others which will delight your family and friends.

The recipes in this book will give you much more control over what you eat. Once you have tried the recipes, you can alter them to specific palates. Any spice—in most any recipe—can be increased, decreased, or eliminated. No longer must you tolerate overspiced, oversalted, fatty sausages, which cost too much, shrivel up in cooking, and are taste-disappointing to boot.

Our products will in no way resemble those sausages made commercially. Ours have no chemical ingredients, are low-fat, low-sodium, but are long on nutrition and good taste.

Once you've made your own sausage, we don't think you'll ever be satisfied with commercial sausage again.

HISTORY OF SAUSAGE

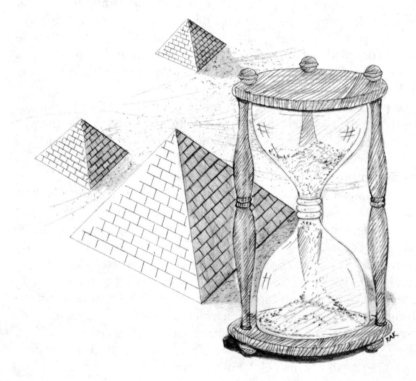

Chapter 1

The common hot dog—a frankfurter tucked in a bun and smothered with onions, pickles, catsup, and mustard—is traditional fare in American ball parks. Equally at home in many corners of the world, this favorite sausage has an illustrious heritage reaching back thousands of years before the birth of Christ to ancient Egypt, Babylon, Greece, and Rome.

In the valley of the Nile, hieroglyphs and simple drawings record the impressive diets of upperclass Egyptians—fruits, vegetables, meats from various breeds of domestic cattle, stuffed game animals, dried fish, and bread in many shapes. These early residents of the Old Kingdom had a well-developed civilization. Their talents engineered and built the great pyramids about 2600 B.C. and it is probable that, just as they ground grain into flour for bread, they chopped meat, added spices, and thus created sausage.

In ancient Greece, the poet Homer set out to write *The Odyssey*, his epic work which details the wanderings of King Odysseus. Written about 800 B.C., this poem contains three references to sausage in the Robert Fitzgerald translations (Anchor Books, 1963):

Gentlemen, quiet! One more thing: here are goat stomachs ready on the fire to stuff with blood and fat, good supper pudding. (page 336)

Now from the fire his fat blood pudding came, deposited by Antinoos—then, to boot, two brown loaves from the basket, and some wine in a fine cup of gold. (page 339)

(Odysseus) rage held hard in leash, submitted to his mind, while he himself rocked, rolling from side to side, as a cook turns a sausage, big with blood and fat, at a scorching blaze,

1

> without a pause, to broil it quick; so he rolled left and right,
> casting about to see how he, alone, against the false outrageous
> crowd of suitors could press the fight. (page 376)

The image of the troubled king, twisting and turning in his
bed like a sausage being broiled over a fire, and the two
references to blood pudding, suggest the integral part sausage
played in ancient Grecian diets.

Across the Ionian Sea, the early Romans had created a variety
of diced meat products and had given them a Latin name.
Salsus translates literally as salted, or preserved, meat, the very
thing we call sausage.

By the time Julius Caesar came upon the scene, sausage was a
staple of the Roman festivals. As the galas got bigger, wilder,
and more extravagant, sausage became more closely identified
with the hoopla, much as turkey is identified with an American
Thanksgiving and plum pudding with British holidays. The
Roman festivals were doomed to extinction when the Christian
era dawned. Banned right along with the fun and games was
sausage.

The Romans, though—like Americans of the 1920s—were not
about to give up one of their favorite foods, Christians or no
Christians. In something akin to Prohibition bootlegging in the
United States, resourceful ancient Roman black-marketeers
organized a sausage distribution system which lasted through
the reigns of several Christian emperors. Eventually, the sausage ban was lifted.

As civilizations arose in other parts of the globe, each seems to
have created some sort of chopped meat product akin to what we
now know as sausage.

The early Britons, and their kinsmen to the north in Scotland,
enjoyed black pudding made of cereal grains ground into meal,
suet, and hog's blood, a product which sounds very much like the
blood pudding described in *The Odyssey.* Another favorite dish
in the early British Isles was white pudding, which consisted of
suet and toasted meal but omitted the hog's blood.

Haggis, now considered a traditional Scottish dish, is also

similar to Homer's blood pudding. Made of finely ground organ meats, suet, and spices which are stuffed into an everted animal stomach, haggis actually debuted in early 15th century English writings before its appearance in Scottish literature.

During the Middle Ages, sausage making became a fine art. People with particular expertise went commercial, opened their own shops, and developed unique products by using special combinations of chopped meats and spices. Before the days of artificial refrigeration, the sausage maker was the daily fast food stop for homemakers seeking inexpensive, nutritious food for the family table.

As sausage popularity grew, new varieties appeared and many of them were named for their place of origin. The Italian city of Bologna gave us the sausage of the same name. Salami is said to have its roots in the Mediterranean community of Salamis, though the word today denotes a type of sausage that is generally further defined by its birthplace—Genoa, Milano, and Sicilian salami from Italy; German and Hungarian salamis from those countries; and Arles salami from France. Göteborg, Sweden, lends its name to a popular semi-dry sausage of the cervelat family. Fresh sausages created in and named for Poland and Italy are particular favorites around the world.

The frankfurter originated in the German city of Frankfurt am Main as early as the 1500s. Called a dry frying sausage, it was made of cured pork and bacon and was a breakfast favorite. This sausage was also dubbed Frankfurter wurst and it differed in size from most sausages of the era. The frankfurter was small, about the size of today's hot dog, rather than large, like bolognas and salamis, and was sliced before serving.

The wiener, or hot dog, evolved from this Frankfurt sausage, according to sources at Union Carbide Corporation.

J. G. Lahner, a German native living in Vienna, is thought to have created the first hot dog about 1800 in his adopted city. He called his sausage Frankfurter wurst, meaning Frankfurt-style sausage, probably for two reasons: Frankfurt was the city of his birth and his sausage was similar in size to the German product. But the sausage that Lahner developed in Vienna, or Wien, to use the city's native name, was altered considerably from the German frankfurter in order to please local palates. The Europeans who tasted it renamed it Wiener wurst but the long name was soon abbreviated to Wiener.

Among the early wiener lovers was the Austrian Princess Pauline Metternich, who set the pattern for eating the tasty new sausage. There, in front of the assembled Austrian aristocracy, the Princess Pauline, with great delicacy, picked up the wiener with her thumb and index finger and gracefully plunked it into her royal mouth.

Decades later, an unknown American apparently saved us from this sticky finger approach to the wiener. The time was 1904, the site the St. Louis World's Fair, which was held in the city's beautiful Forest Park. A sausage vendor, bowing to the niceties of proper eating and concerned with cleanliness and hygiene, served each wiener with a white glove. The thought struck him that buns would be better—cheaper and more appealing. For some unexplained reason, the sign over the vendor's stand read "hot dog," probably used more in the nature of an exclamation meaning "great product," or "good eating." Or perhaps the vendor had indeed christened his own creation. At any rate, the wiener tucked in a bun became what the sign proclaimed, a hot dog.

Just as the bread-wrapped wiener evolved in large part from the vestiges of Victorian table manners, sausages from other cultures depended on climate, on ethnic traditions, and most basically, on the foods and spices available.

The hazards of food spoilage have been with us down through the ages but even primitive peoples understood the basics of preservation. Cooking and smoking were known to enhance the keeping qualities of food but people in the northern regions soon realized that cold weather deterred spoilage. Thus residents of the northern climes developed the smoked and cooked sausages, and the semi-dry summer sausages which were made in the winter for warm-weather consumption.

In the warmer parts of the world, people had learned that sun drying acted to preserve food and from these areas came the dried sausages which need no refrigeration.

Ethnic considerations also determined the types of sausage which evolved from a particular culture. Certain religious traditions and dietary laws proscribed the consumption of various foods, so substitutions were made.

In addition, the available foods and spices developed the taste buds of a particular culture. Primitive peoples wrapped their food in leaves to keep the fire's dust and ash from it. In the process, they realized the leaves imparted a different, often more pleasant, taste to their food. Most of the spices originated in the East, and the early Babylonian, Greek, and Roman civilizations are known to have added flavorful leaves, seeds, and berries to their meats. As those civilizations spread westward, the knowledge of spices went with them. Interest in seasonings, among other things, prompted the great sea journeys which led explorers to the New World.

Eastern and Iberian palates tolerated more spice, so sausages from Spain, Italy, Portugal, and the Mediterranean region tend to be hot and spicy. Middle European sausages are less seasoned and those from Great Britain are even more bland.

The local potable often found its way into sausage, too. The Germans added beer; the Italians wine.

With the spread of the early civilizations, the opening of the sea routes, and the development of the spice trade, great immigrations began. Throughout the years, people coming to the New World from the British Isles, from Europe, Iberia, the Middle East, and the Orient brought with them their heritage, as many possessions as they could manage, and their ethnic foods, among them the sausages of their lands.

Purists believe that sausage, to be sausage, must be encased, but by definition, the product is simply comminuted, or chopped, seasoned meat. When the early immigrants arrived in the New World they discovered the North American Indians eating a meat dish called pemmican. Made of chopped dried meat seasoned with dried berries, the product was shaped into patties rather than stuffed into casings. The early American pioneers also made pemmican in jerky-like strips which were easily preserved and transported.

Another chopped-meat product, scrapple or panhas, is said to have originated with the German immigrants who settled in Pennsylvania and were dubbed the Pennsylvania Dutch, a corruption of the proper term Pennsylvania Deutsch. Made of ground pork trimmings, cornmeal, stock, and spices, scrapple is chilled and then sliced and fried. If oatmeal is substituted for the cornmeal, the dish is often called goetta.

The immigrants also adapted their own recipes to the kinds of food and spices available in the new land. Many of the old favorites took on unique new flavors and textures.

As in the Middle Ages, those sausage makers with particular expertise went commercial and opened up sausage kitchens and little shops to provide their less talented friends and neighbors with good-tasting, nutritious, and inexpensive meals.

The popularity of sausage increased and with it grew the demand for more. To help meet the sausage needs of a burgeoning populace, new machines were created to speed up the chopping, grinding, mixing, and stuffing operations. And, as more sausage became available, more people came to know and love this ancient favorite. The advent of artificial refrigeration and refrigerated railroad cars and trucks further aided distribution of sausage, thus creating still more sausage lovers.

The animal casing industry, though, was hard put to keep up with the demand as the popularity of sausage continued to grow. Worse yet, because of its international scope, it was subject to fluctuating world events—war, natural disasters, and economic woes.

In 1916, Erwin O. Freund, an American who had been in the animal casing business all his life, dreamed of developing man-made sausage casings. Such a product, made cheaply in uniform sizes, and strong enough to withstand the commercial stuffing operation, would revolutionize the sausage industry.

To make his dream come true, Freund set up a research fellowship at the Mellon Institute. Early work there pointed to cellulose as the potential synthetic casing.

The investigation was carried on by W. F. Henderson and H. E. Dietrich, and in 1925 a man-made, commercially marketable, inedible sausage casing became available. Freund's dream had become a reality with a bonus—when he stripped the synthetic casing from the meat he discovered the product retained its shape even without the casing. The skinless frank was born.

Other people working in different places developed another man-made casing using the interior side of cattle hides. Edible collagen casings are also strong and even sized but, like cellulose casings, they are difficult to come by in small quantities and are used primarily in commercial sausage production.

The various lunch meats on the market, while not strictly sausages, are certainly derivatives of the sausage family. They, too, have processed, minced meat as a base, plus spices, herbs and possibly cheese, olives, pimientos or even pickles in them. To distinguish them from sausage, they are called cooked meat specialties and generally appear in loaf or sandwich spread forms.

Still other processed meats, called prepared meat products, come in pasteurized form as fully cooked hams, which are kept under refrigeration, or on supermarket shelves in sterilized forms as sandwich meats or corned beef hash.

Through the ages, sausage has been a favorite food in many cultures. Its popularity is still growing and its production is returning to the home where it originated.

SIX BASIC SAUSAGE GROUPS

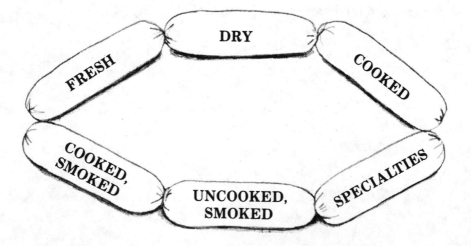

FRESH

DRY

COOKED

COOKED, SMOKED

UNCOOKED, SMOKED

SPECIALTIES

Chapter 2

Omit the garlic from a sausage recipe and you have a totally different product. Add chili powder to a bland sausage recipe and you've created another entirely new item.

Because the addition or subtraction of a single element results in a completely different product with its own unique taste, sausages are classified not by their ingredients but by how they are made.

The American Meat Institute classifies sausage into the following groups:

Fresh
Uncooked, smoked
Cooked
Cooked, smoked
Dry
Cooked meat specialties

Fresh sausage is exactly what its name implies—sausage made from meat that has not been cooked, smoked, or cured in any way. The sausages made from recipes in this book all belong to the fresh sausage group. Bratwurst and pork sausage, for example, are fresh sausages.

All products in this group must be refrigerated before cooking and cooked thoroughly before serving.

Uncooked, smoked sausage is similar to fresh sausage except that the uncooked meats have been cured first and then smoked. The smoking process imparts the special taste and color to this group of sausages. Smoked country-style pork sausage, mettwurst, and Polish sausage are among the most popular uncooked, smoked sausage varieties.

Like fresh sausage, sausage in this group must also be kept refrigerated and cooked thoroughly before serving.

Cooked sausage is generally made from fresh, uncured meats which are ground and blended with spices and then cooked before distribution to the consumer. In some cases, cured meats are used but the end product is still cooked before distribution. Sausages in this group may also be smoked but the smoking takes place after the cooking process and is used simply to impart the smoky flavor. Liver sausage, beerwurst, cotto salami, and liver cheese are favorites in the cooked sausage category.

Since the sausages in this group have already been fully cooked, they are considered ready-to-eat and usually are served cold.

Fresh meats that have been smoked and fully cooked are used to make products in the cooked, smoked sausage group. The world's two most popular sausages, frankfurters and bologna, are members of this group, as are knackwurst and smokies or smoked links.

Having been fully cooked, these sausages are also ready to eat but their flavor is generally enhanced if they are heated in some way before serving. They should be kept refrigerated until using.

Sausages in the dry sausage group come in two varieties: dry, or hard, and a semi-dry product, which is softer. Both are prepared in a carefully controlled, highly technical environment because bacterial fermentation is part of the production process.

Hard sausages are mostly members of the salami family. Air drying for up to six months removes about half the moisture in them, which shrivels the casings and hardens the texture. The manufacturing process makes these sausages ready-to-eat though they are not cooked.

Some salamis (see Glossary) are cooked sausages, rather than dry sausages, which have been partially dried after cooking. Sausages in this group must be kept refrigerated, though salamis in the dry sausage family need only cold storage.

The semi-dry group of sausages, mostly cervelats or "summer sausages," are partially dried in the smokehouse but fully cooked. They have a softer texture than the hard sausages and should be kept under refrigeration until serving. They can be eaten cold or heated according to individual tastes.

Cooked meat specialties encompass items such as sandwich spreads, lunch meats, luncheon loaves, and meat products bound by gelatinous or jellied substances. They consist of fully cooked chopped meat and spices, and may contain cheese, olives, pimientos, or other tangy morsels.

All cooked meat specialties are ready-to-eat and must be refrigerated until serving. Among the most popular members of this group are ham and cheese loaf, honey loaf, jellied corned beef and headcheese.

Finally, a word about prepared meats. These are not sausages, but cuts of meats that have undergone some sort of processing before distribution to the consumer. They can be cooked, cured, or smoked. The most common prepared meat product is ham, most of which is cured, molded, steam or water cooked, and generally referred to as "boiled ham."

Two processing methods distinguish canned meat products. Those which have been pasteurized need refrigeration and are found in the meat or delicatessen section of the supermarket. Canned hams are the most popular pasteurized meat product.

The canned meats found on the supermarket shelves have been sterilized, rather than pasteurized, and need no refrigeration until they are opened. Corned beef hash and canned luncheon meats are popular choices of consumers using sterile prepared meat products.

EQUIPMENT FOR MAKING SAUSAGE AT HOME

Chapter 3

The ordinary household kitchen probably contains all the tools you need to make tantalizing sausage for family and friends—sharp knives, a small scale, and a meat grinder. For those purists who believe sausage in *patty* form is "nothing more than hamburger," a stuffer for loading the meat into casings is a handy tool.

Knives

Good quality cutlery, though not inexpensive, is a boon to any efficient kitchen, but only two good knives—a five-inch boner to separate meat from bone and a ten-inch breaking knife to cut the meat into workable chunks—are essential to the art of sausage making.

A good knife combines quality steel, a cutting blade professionally honed to razor sharpness, and a comfortable handle, which holds the tang (the part of the blade that extends into the handle) and adds balance to the instrument.

Most knives are made of carbon steel, stainless steel, or a combination of both. A good blade, a marriage of these two principal elements, is labeled high carbon stainless steel.

Thousands of microscopic teeth make up the sharp edge of a good knife. Though there are several types of edges, most professional cooks prefer a standard V-grind because it slices quickly and neatly without excess drag of the blade.

As we've mentioned, the knife tang is the back end of the blade which extends into the handle. A full tang, running the length and width of the handle, is secured by three rivets and adds weight and balance to the product. Knives also may have half tangs, secured with two rivets, a round or rat-tail tang, or a narrow flat tongue called a drive tang.

On some decorative cutlery, such as carving sets, the blade and the handle may be forged as a single piece. Most knives, however, are made in two pieces, with handles of china, plastic, wood, bone, or plasticized wood.

Very tight bonding of the individual knife pieces is essential to keep bacteria from breeding at the junctures and to prevent separate movement of the parts, which reduces efficiency and can cause dangerous slippage.

All good knives, of course, demand proper care.

First, they should be kept sharp. It is dull knives that create problems, not sharp ones.

Knives should also be stored in a protective sleeve, either a knife block or in the cardboard or plastic sheaths in which they are delivered. A knife block will protect the cutting edge and the flat sleeves for knives stored in drawers will protect not only the cutting surface but will also save searching fingers from injury.

The cutting edge of the knife, the essence of the instrument, is susceptible to water, heat, and hard surfaces. Each use of the knife will dull the edge somewhat. To prevent excessive dullness, a knife should be used only against a wooden surface. Striking metal, glass, ceramic, or Formica will take its toll on the edge.

Even though instructions from the manufacturer permit dishwasher cleaning of the knife, it is far better to wash a good instrument by hand and dry it immediately. In a dishwasher, the heat, the impact of the water against the knife, and of the knife against other objects will all dull the edge. In addition, the temperature and water will eventually affect the handle's looks and possibly loosen the bond between the handle and the tang, creating room for bacteria to breed.

Even with proper care, ordinary use will dull a knife's cutting edge. While electric knife sharpeners are popular small-appliance adjuncts, they are not the best instruments for sharpening quality knives. It is better to use a sharpening steel which, while not actually "sharpening" the edge, will properly realign the tiny teeth which comprise it.

The hardness of the steel's composition determines the size of the teeth it will restore to the edge—small, medium, or large The tooth size in turn depends on the type of meat to be cut. A medium-grain sharpening steel will put a general purpose edge on a household knife.

Using a sharpening steel will keep a knife in workable condition for one to three years, depending on the quality of the knife itself, its usage and the care it is given. Eventually however, the edge will have to be reground—a highly skilled job better left to a professional grinder.

Scales

An inexpensive nondiet kitchen scale is a handy tool for measuring the correct ratio of meat to fat in your sausage recipes.

Kitchen scales come in three basic styles—one whose weighing surface is a flat top, or platform; one which also includes some sort of container which fits on the weighing platform; and one which features a container hanging below the dial, much like the old-time grocery store produce scales. All of these scales should have dials which enable you to disallow the weight of a container in measuring ingredients in the container. For instance, you should be able to place your half-pound plastic container on the weighing surface and turn the dial back to zero so the scale will weigh only what is in the container and not the container itself.

Most scales have a weighing capacity of five to twenty-five pounds, with increments in ounces or in quarter-pounds. The newer scales which mount on the wall and which have a fold-down weighing surface generally have smaller capacities—about ten pounds—so they will not be torn from the wall.

To sum up, a good scale can be adjusted to disallow the weight of a container and has an easy-to-read dial and a weighing surface capability of at least five pounds in one-ounce increments.

Meat Grinders

Basically three types of meat grinder are on the market today: manual grinders, which attach to a table or a counter top, electric grinders, which are single-purpose small appliances, and grinder attachments for kitchen mixers.

In each instance, the L-shaped device has an entrance hopper at the vertical top and an exit opening at the horizontal end. Grinders consist of a four-bladed, X-shaped cutting knife, at least two grinder plates—one with holes about $\frac{3}{16}$ inch in diameter for fine grinding, and another whose holes are about $\frac{3}{8}$ inch in diameter for a coarser grind—and a worm which propels the meat from the hopper through the knife and the grinder plate. A wooden plunger is also included with many grinders to push the food through the hopper to the worm.

In order to accommodate a sausage stuffer, the horizontal exit opening of any grinder must have a threaded collar which keeps the works together. Older models, which have wing nuts at the horizontal end, preclude the addition of the stuffer to the grinder.

Meat also may be ground in a food processor but extreme care must be taken. Because of the machine's speed, the meat may quickly be over-processed into something like a paté—much too fine-textured for ordinary sausage.

In general, a device built specifically to grind meat is a good sausage-making investment. If, however, you would prefer that the device be an attachment to your kitchen mixer, check before you buy to see if the purchase of an additional power pack to accommodate the attachment is necessary. It may be less expensive to buy a free-standing grinder—either manual or electric—than a grinder attachment *and* a power pack for your mixer.

Stuffers

A sausage stuffer is nothing more than a metal or plastic funnel with a fairly wide hopper end and a narrow neck whose exit is about $\frac{3}{4}$ inch in diameter.

Stuffers that attach to grinders or grinder attachments will have narrower hoppers because they do not have to accommodate fingers forcing the meat through them.

Small manual stuffers, similar to meat grinders, are available but they are rather expensive and a good investment only if you plan to make a lot of sausage on a regular basis. Even smaller manual stuffers may turn up in your local antique store. Made of metal, the body of these stuffers is about 10 inches long and resembles a curved piece of pipe. A hinged pusher/handle is attached to the hopper end of the instrument, which narrows to the stuffer nozzle at the exit end. The stuffer sits on the table on back legs about three inches high and front legs that are just above the surface.

Sausage stuffers may also exist where you least expect them. A pastry bag will work if the cone is long enough to accommodate a length of casing and the opening is wide enough to permit fairly fast exiting of the sausage meat. A cookie press with the same qualifications will also double as a sausage stuffer.

Home Smokers

The continuing popularity of outdoor cooking has spawned a product line of smokers which, in addition to very slow cooking, also impart a tangy smoke flavor to food.

These smokers come in two varieties: water smokers, which are meant primarily to flavor food, and dry smokers which accomplish the longer smoking-to-preserve process, a process which demands brining.

Designed similarly, both products come in single and double grill form; are heated either electrically or by charcoal; have loose-fitting covers which allow the smoke to escape and create a draft; have built-in temperature gauges to monitor the interior heat; and have a container for the wood chips which provide the smoke. In addition, water smokers include a pan which, when filled with water, acts as a self-baster, keeping the meat moist throughout the cooking process. Adding beer, wine, juice, herbs, or spices to the water further enhances the flavor of the smoked foods.

Because smoking-to-flavor and smoking-to-preserve are both fairly lengthy processes, a door near the smoker's heat source is essential. This simplifies the addition of more hardwood chips, and charcoal for nonelectric smokers, during cooking, and reduces the risk of accidents in having to move the food section, or the food and water sections, off the heat source when adding chips or charcoal.

Generally speaking, nonelectric smokers can also be used as grills. Those heated electrically, however, may have elements incapable of producing enough heat to be as versatile.

Homemade Smokers

It is easy, fun, and inexpensive to build a smoker in your backyard. Not only will the smoker add interesting new flavors to food, it will also intrigue the neighbors and help keep the mosquitoes away.

The device must have four essential elements: 1) a source for the fire and smoke; 2) a housing of some sort to contain the smoke; 3) racks or hooks to hold the food being smoked; and, 4) a top vent through which moisture and smoke escape and which creates the draft to pull fire-sustaining air and smoke through the apparatus.

Smokers with removable tops, through which the food is placed inside, also need a piece of wood to keep the top about an inch above the receptacle itself and a piece of thin cloth, or cheesecloth, to keep insects out.

Permanent smokehouses appear on many farms, in seashore communities, and in small villages and towns. They are usually made of brick or concrete block and, though they vary in size, are often only six or seven feet square and about seven feet high. Their fire pit may be directly beneath the food racks or it may be some distance away and have a trench which conveys the smoke from the fire source to the smokehouse.

Other smokers can be made from 50-gallon whiskey barrels, oil drums, or even old refrigerators or upright freezers if they have metal interior parts rather than plastic ones.

Generally, you can build homemade smokers for less than $30 and in short order it will become a family project for the cook, the tinkerer, and the kids who can play with fire under parental supervision.

Making a Barrel Smoker

A 50-gallon whiskey barrel, which reeked of a Kentucky distiller's product, became our smoker. It was definitely a used barrel, an attribute essential to the cooking process. We decided that if the barrel would hold aging liquid spirits, it would certainly hold the smoke necessary to the cooking operation.

A leakproof barrel is sealed by six metal bands which hold the staves and both ends together. In order to convert the barrel to a smoker, it is necessary to remove its ends one at a time.

First, remove the top steel band by placing a pry bar or a large screwdriver at the edge of the band so the tool is at right angles to the band itself. Using a hammer, firmly rap the tool and work your way around the band so that it loosens and moves toward the barrel end. Repeat the procedure on the second band from that end, until it too comes off and the end of the barrel is released. Replace both steel bands and turn the barrel over to repeat the removal process at the opposite end.

It is essential to replace the two steel bands at one end of the barrel before starting to remove the two at the opposite end. A barrel with four bands off may become nothing more than a heap of wooden staves, heavy ends, and circles of metal lying in your back yard.

To monitor the heat in the barrel, a roast meat thermometer is inserted in a hole, matching the diameter of the thermometer probe, which has been drilled through the barrel bung—the removable "cork" which accommodates the distiller's testing tap.

About six feet from the spot for which our barrel was destined, we dug a fire pit two feet square and one foot deep. From the pit to the barrel site, an upward-sloping trench about six inches deep and six inches wide provided for the flow of smoke from the pit to the barrel. The barrel was then centered over the end of the trench.

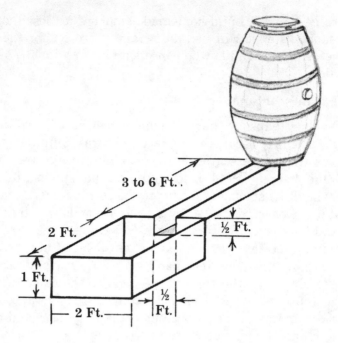

Next, we placed a piece of sheet metal, large enough to cover, over the fire pit and covered the trench with a length of board. Because the board effectively sealed the trench, it was not necessary to mound dirt around it to prevent smoke leakage.

Wooden slats about one inch square were placed across the top of the barrel. The sausages are hung from the slats during the smoking operation. Once destined to be tomato stakes, we used these pieces of scrap lumber because the broomsticks and dowel rods we tried rolled around the top of the barrel—since the barrel itself was not absolutely level.

One end of the barrel becomes excess baggage but during the smoking process the other end is positioned atop the slats, which results in an air space. Over that, we placed a thin piece of cloth, or cheesecloth, which hangs partway down the barrel and keeps insects from wandering into the smoker.

When the fire is lighted and the smoke is being produced, the sheet metal covering the fire pit is raised along the edge which faces the wind, to provide the air necessary to support the fire. Thus vented, the smoke is drawn from the fire pit through the trench into the barrel itself and out the top.

INGREDIENTS

Chapter 4

Meat

The meats you use in sausage making will depend largely on your lifestyle—on whether you live in a city or suburb, in a small town, or on a farm, and whether you're a pork lover or prefer beef, lamb, or veal.

Supermarket shoppers should watch for meat sales, particularly for pork sales, since pork is a prime ingredient in so many sausage recipes.

The pork cuts that we use in sausage making are derived either from pork shoulders or pork loins. Sometimes the center pork loin is used but only when this cut of meat sells for less than shoulder or end cuts. The quality and flavor of sausage made from center pork loin is outstanding.

The best value comes from buying a whole loin of pork. This will provide chops, back ribs, roasts, and cutlets, while the ends can be ground into sausage meat. A whole loin costing twenty dollars can double in value after it is cut into smaller pieces at home.

Fresh picnics (shoulder of pork) and hams can also be used for sausage but they are rarely found in supermarkets because most of them are smoked or cured before retail distribution. The same is true of pork bellies. They could also become sausage meat, but are usually processed into bacon and not available fresh to the consumer.

Residents of rural areas who have whole hogs butchered for their own use can reserve the most suitable parts of the animals for grinding into sausage meat. All pork meat has the same tenderness; the meat varies only in the degree of fat and bone. Sausage can be made from any part not used for other serving purposes.

PORK   CHART

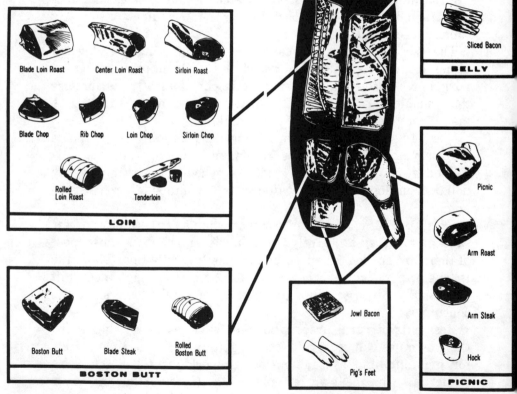

Pork Chart (Photo Courtesy United States Department of Agriculture)

PORK CUTS

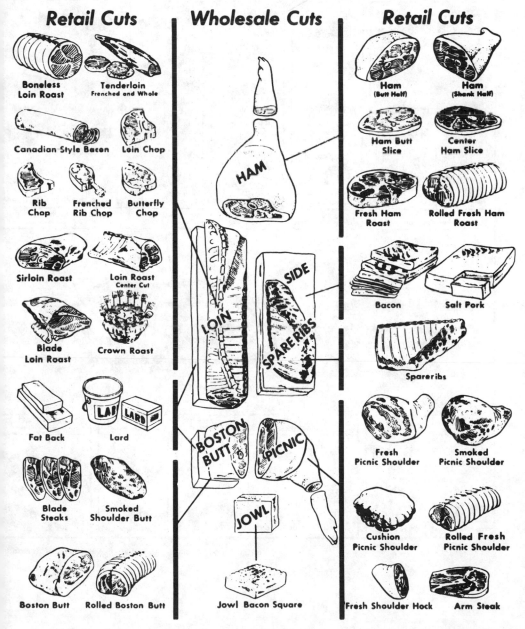

Retail Cuts

Boneless Loin Roast
Tenderloin Frenched and Whole

Canadian Style Bacon
Loin Chop

Rib Chop
Frenched Rib Chop
Butterfly Chop

Sirloin Roast
Loin Roast Center Cut

Blade Loin Roast
Crown Roast

Fat Back
Lard

Blade Steaks
Smoked Shoulder Butt

Boston Butt
Rolled Boston Butt

Wholesale Cuts

HAM

LOIN

SIDE

SPARE RIBS

BOSTON BUTT

PICNIC

JOWL

Retail Cuts

Ham (Butt Half)
Ham (Shank Half)

Ham Butt Slice
Center Ham Slice

Fresh Ham Roast
Rolled Fresh Ham Roast

Bacon
Salt Pork

Spareribs

Fresh Picnic Shoulder
Smoked Picnic Shoulder

Cushion Picnic Shoulder
Rolled Fresh Picnic Shoulder

Jowl Bacon Square

Fresh Shoulder Hock
Arm Steak

Pork Cuts (Photo Courtesy United States Department of Agriculture)

BEEF CHART

RETAIL CUTS OF BEEF — WHERE THEY COME FROM AND HOW TO COOK THEM

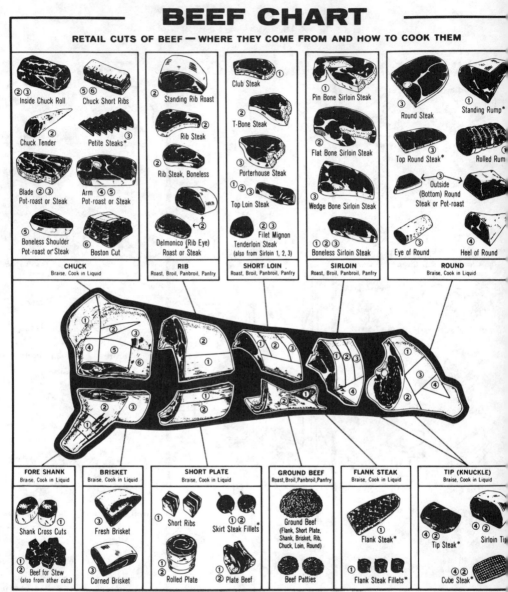

CHUCK
Braise, Cook in Liquid

②③ Inside Chuck Roll
⑤⑥ Chuck Short Ribs
② Chuck Tender
③ Petite Steaks*
Blade ②③ Pot-roast or Steak
Arm ④⑤ Pot-roast or Steak
⑤ Boneless Shoulder Pot-roast or Steak
⑥ Boston Cut

RIB
Roast, Broil, Panbroil, Panfry

② Standing Rib Roast
② Rib Steak
② Rib Steak, Boneless
②↔② Delmonico (Rib Eye) Roast or Steak

SHORT LOIN
Roast, Broil, Panbroil, Panfry

Club Steak ①
② T-Bone Steak
③ Porterhouse Steak
①②③ Top Loin Steak
②③ Filet Mignon Tenderloin Steak (also from Sirloin 1, 2, 3)

SIRLOIN
Roast, Broil, Panbroil, Panfry

① Pin Bone Sirloin Steak
Flat Bone Sirloin Steak
③ Wedge Bone Sirloin Steak
①②③ Boneless Sirloin Steak

ROUND
Braise, Cook in Liquid

③ Round Steak
① Standing Rump*
③ Top Round Steak*
Rolled Rum
③ Outside (Bottom) Round Steak or Pot-roast
③ Eye of Round
④ Heel of Round

FORE SHANK
Braise, Cook in Liquid

① Shank Cross Cuts
①② Beef for Stew (also from other cuts)

BRISKET
Braise, Cook in Liquid

③ Fresh Brisket
③ Corned Brisket

SHORT PLATE
Braise, Cook in Liquid

① Short Ribs
①② Skirt Steak Fillets*
①② Rolled Plate
① ② Plate Beef

GROUND BEEF
Roast, Broil, Panbroil, Panfry

Ground Beef (Flank, Short Plate, Shank, Brisket, Rib, Chuck, Loin, Round)
Beef Patties

FLANK STEAK
Braise, Cook in Liquid

① Flank Steak*
①② Flank Steak Fillets*

TIP (KNUCKLE)
Braise, Cook in Liquid

④② Tip Steak*
④② Sirloin Ti
④② Cube Steak*

* May be Roasted, Broiled, Panbroiled or Panfried from high quality beef.

Beef Chart (Photo Courtesy United States Department of Agricultu

STANDARD RETAIL BEEF CUTS

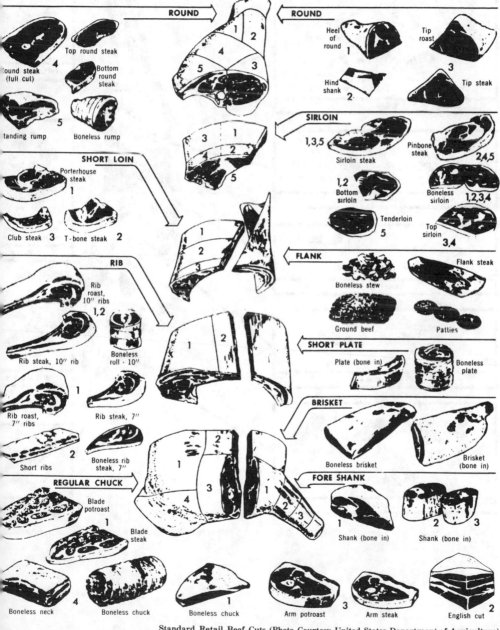

Standard Retail Beef Cuts (Photo Courtesy United States Department of Agriculture)

LAMB   CHART

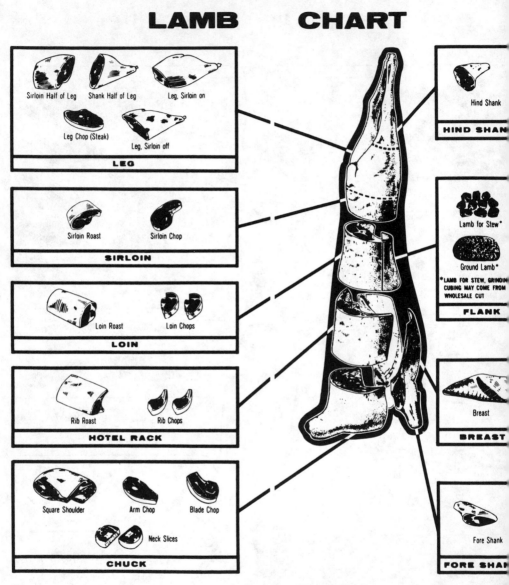

Lamb Chart (Photo Courtesy United States Department of Agricult

In commercial sausage processing, every part of the hog is used, including the head and the trimmings—those scraps that accumulate from butchering the animal into retail cuts.

There is less versatility in choosing beef for sausage making and most often it will be beef chuck which is used. For those who have access to sides of beef, the plate and the brisket can also be ground into sausage meat. It doesn't pay to use steaks, which are akin to pork loin, because of their prohibitive price.

Because both lamb and veal meats are expensive, too, it is essential to watch for special sales. In our recipes we have used only breasts and shoulders for sausage making. If there are no other purposes for the shanks, especially the foreshanks, they too can be used, but they must be ground twice to break down tissue and muscle.

Casings

Commercial sausage makers have three casing options open to them: inedible cellulose casings and the edible collagen and natural casings.

Natural casings are derived from the stomachs, bladders, and intestines of meat-producing animals, principally beef cattle, sheep, and hogs. Those of us who make sausage at home are usually restricted to pork casings since these are the only ones readily available on the retail market. In some rare instances, you can order sheep casings through your butcher. Though tender and delicious, sheep casings are small and difficult to stuff by hand because the proper size stuffing funnels are not available for retail sale.

Years ago, muslin bags were also used for molding sausage. Today plastic wrap and aluminum foil have made muslin bags— which had to be sewed, and washed, and dried—unnecessary.

The casings used in our recipes are all natural pork casings because they are inexpensive, readily available, and the easiest to use without special, hard-to-find stuffing funnels.

Spices

Like sausage itself, the use of spices in food preparation goes back thousands of years before the birth of Christ. The earliest people wrapped leaves around their meat to protect it from ashes in the cook process and learned that interesting new flavors resulted.

Since ancient times, man has used spices for a variety of other purposes as well—for making wines, for personal fragrances, for medicinal preparations, and in religious rituals.

Spice traders often accumulated great wealth and in early cultures people connived, married, and even killed to obtain spice and to keep their spice sources a secret from competitors.

It was search for spices that spawned many of the great explorations—Marco Polo's journey to the East, the voyages of Christopher Columbus, Vasco da Gama, and Ferdinand Magellan. And spices today remain an important part of our lives. They provide variety, interest, and appeal to foods which might otherwise be dull and lacking in flavor.

We tend to think of all seasonings as spices when actually some are herbs, a subtle difference.

Spices are the dried fruit, flowers, bark, roots, seeds, or buds of plants that usually are native to tropical areas. Herbs are generally the leaves, and sometimes the flowers, of plants that grow primarily in temperate climates. Herbs are available in fresh or dry forms.

Seeds are whole, or parts of whole fruit and/or seeds and come in either fresh or dried form. Blends are a combination of one or more spices, herbs, and seeds.

Because personal tastes vary greatly, the discriminating use of herbs and spices is essential. Seasonings of all kinds should be used in moderation. Once added to food, seasoning cannot be removed and it is impossible to correct an undesirable taste once one has developed. On the other hand, additions are easy to make if the original amounts are inadequate.

In our recipes, we suggest tasting sausage samples to correct seasonings. But it is essential to remember that before tasting, the meat must be thoroughly cooked since so many sausages contain pork.

Seasonings are intended to enhance flavors rather than mask them, except in those few situations that call for a predominant flavor.

It's wise to buy spices in the smallest amounts possible, preferably at specialty or health food stores where they are available in bulk. Many spices, especially ground ones, lose their pungency and fragrance in three months' time. After that, it is best to discard the remainder, particularly if it has lost its special aroma. Whole spices, such as nutmeg and peppercorns, will keep their flavor for a longer period of time.

In addition to dating spices when they are purchased, keep them tightly covered and stored in a cool, dry place to ensure freshness. All herbs and spices require cooking to develop their aromatic essence.

To truly appreciate the unique characteristics of individual herbs, you can grow your own herb garden in your yard, in a window box, or on your kitchen window sill. Herbs grow easily, particularly in a south window, and they do not need a lot of attention. Herb gardens are sometimes available in complete kits, but seeds for rosemary, tarragon, savory, thyme, basil, marjoram, chives, mint, and dill can be bought in individual packages.

Home grown herbs will greatly enchance your cooking and the flavors are much better than from herbs which are commercially processed.

The following are the principal herbs and spices used in our sausage recipes:

Allspice *(Pimenta dioica)*—also called Jamaica Pimenta, allspice is grown almost exclusively in the Western Hemisphere. Though it resembles a blend of cloves, cinnamon, and nutmeg, it is not a combination of the three but a spice of its own. Careful use of allspice is important, as it intensifies on standing.

Basil *(Ocimum basilicum)*—Grown in the northern Mediterranean areas but native to India, basil can even be cultivated in window boxes. It is very pungent in fresh form but loses much of its fragrance when dry. Basil has a sweet, clove-like taste.

Bay Leaves *(Laurus nobilis)*—Sometimes referred to as laurel leaves, bay leaves are grown in Asia Minor, the Mediterranean area, and in the western United States. They have a pungent, distinctive taste, which can become bitter. Dried bay leaves have an almost lemony aroma.

Caraway Seeds *(Carum carvi)*—Native to Europe, Asia, and North Africa and grown extensively in the Netherlands, caraway seed is from a plant of the parsley family and has a distinct flavor and aroma.

Celery Seed *(Apium graveolens)*—Usually imported to this country from India and France, celery seed provides the aromatic characteristics of fresh celery. In Europe, celery seed is known as "smallage."

Chili Powder—Actually a blend of spices which will vary by brand name, chili powder is of American origin. This is one flavoring used to dominate others. It is generally a blend of chili peppers, cumin, garlic, and oregano.

Chives *(Allium schoenoprasum)*—A delicate member of the onion family, chives will grow in window boxes and can be seen popping up annually with the earliest spring flowers.

Cinnamon *(Cinnamomum zeylanicum)*—Sometimes called cassia, cinnamon is the inner bark of an evergreen tree of the laurel family. Reddish brown in color, it is distinctively sweet, slightly pungent, and lends a spicy flavor to food. Cinnamon is grown in Sri Lanka, southeast Asia, and Indonesia.

Clove *(Eugenia caryophyllata)*—Native to the Moluccas in eastern Indonesia and also imported to the U.S. from Zanzibar, clove should be used sparingly. Its flavor intensifies upon standing and it has a sharp, pungent taste and a fragrant aroma.

Coriander *(Coriandrum sativum)*—The dried fruit or seed of the coriander plant, part of the parsley family, this seasoning is native to the Mediterranean region but it is now grown around the world. Coriander is light brown in color and has a strong, sweet, nutty aroma. It is piquant in taste.

Cumin *(Cuminum cyminum)*—Also called comino, cumin is

imported here from Iran and Morocco. It has a strong flavor, mostly nutty in taste, and should be used sparingly.

Curry Powder—A blend of many spices, curry powder will vary according to the supplier. It can include chili, coriander, cinnamon, turmeric, mustard, cloves, and pepper. Available in both hot and mild varieties, curry powder is a staple of Indian cookery. It is pungent and used to dominate rather than enhance flavors.

Dill *(Anethum graveolens)*—Native to Europe, imported to this country from India but also grown in California, dill is the seeds or leaves of a plant of the parsley family. It possesses a characteristic flavor that is pungent and aromatic, lending itself well to bland foods.

Fennel *(Foeniculum vulgare)*—Native to the Mediterranean region, fennel has a sweet licorice flavor, not unlike anise, with a distinct, appealing aroma. When fennel is not available, anise may be substituted since its characteristics are similar.

Garlic *(Allium sativum)*—Grown worldwide, garlic is available in many forms—powder, minced, liquid, and salt. It must be used sparingly as its taste is strong and pungent. Also readily available, fresh garlic is preferable to the processed forms as it provides a milder and more pleasant flavor. Fresh garlic is often used in combination with onions.

Ginger *(Zingiber officinale)*—Native to and exported from southeast Asia and Jamaica, ginger has a hot, spicy, sweet flavor and is derived from the root of the ginger plant. Fresh gingerroot is becoming more widely available in supermarkets because of the popularity of Chinese cooking, in which it is often used.

Juniper*(Juniperus communus)*—Juniper berries are the dried fruit of an evergreen bush. They are slightly bittersweet and are always used in the production of gin.

Lemon *(Citrus limon)*—Lemon is grown in all subtropic regions of the world. Its peel adds a distinctive flavor to a product, varying in its potency by its freshness and type. This is also true for orange peel *(Citrus sinenis)*.

Mace *(Myristica fragrans)*—Mace is the shell of the nutmeg. Mace and nutmeg are both parts of the same fruit but they cannot necessarily be interchanged since mace has a pungent aroma but is stronger than nutmeg. Mace lends a distinctive flavor if not used prudently.

Marjoram *(Majorana hortensis)*—A member of the mint family, marjoram should be used with care until it is quite familiar. While marjoram has a pleasant flavor, it can also impart a bitter taste.

Mint *(Mentha spicata)*—Native to Europe and Asia, mint is readily grown everywhere. It has a sweet aromatic flavor with a cool aftertaste and dominates other flavorings.

Mustard *(Brassica hirta; Brassica nigra)*—Grown in temperate regions, mustard is an annual herb with two varieties. Both yellow and brown seeds are combined to make dry mustard. The yellow variety is used for mustard seed. Pungent in flavor, mustard should be used sparingly.

Nutmeg *(Myristica fragrans)*—Grown in hot, moist climates of the tropics, Indonesia, and the West Indies, nutmeg is the dried seed of an evergreen tree. Its flavor is sweet, spicy, and enhancing. It is used extensively in commercial sausage making, baked products, and a great variety of other foods.

Onion *(Allium cepa)*—A member of the lily family and available in many forms, onions date back to Babylonian times. They are presently used in cooking all over the world and their flavor is familiar to everyone.

Oregano *(Origanum vulgare)*—Similar to marjoram but stronger and more aromatic, oregano possesses a bitter but appealing flavor. Today, its wide use in Italian cookery has made it well known.

Paprika *(Capsicum annuum)*—Paprika's source is the pod of a sweet red pepper. It is grown extensively in California, but is also imported to the U.S. from Spain and central Europe. Supermarket paprika is commonly a sweet paprika. Hot paprika is also available. Used reasonably, paprika provides distinctive color and flavor to sausages and is an excellent source of vitamins A and C.

Parsley *(Petroselinum crispum)*—Two varieties of parsley—plain leafy and curly—can be grown anywhere. Parsley lends flavor and color to many foods. Its flavor is pleasant and mild, and permits its blending with all but sweet products. Vitamin C and minerals are parsley's bonus.

Pepper *(Piper nigrum)*—Native to the East Indies and exported from India, Malaysia, and Indonesia, pepper is the berry of a climbing vine. Its flavor is universally familiar. Freshly ground peppercorns provide the best essence and are more desirable since pepper quickly loses its flavor in ground form. Both white and black peppercorns are available. White peppercorns provide a more aesthetic appearance in light-colored foods and are less pungent than black pepper.

Red Pepper *(Capsicum frutescens)*—The terms red pepper and cayenne are used interchangeably but its quantity in use is controversial. The use of cayenne is purely a personal taste, but too much can produce a numbing taste which overpowers all other ingredients. Wield cayenne carefully.

Poultry Seasoning—A blend of herbs and spices, poultry seasoning varies in its content from supplier to supplier. It is usually composed of sage, thyme, and marjoram plus other spices. Reading the label is important to determine the blend.

Rosemary *(Rosmarinus officinalis)*—Grown in California, Virginia, and North Carolina, rosemary is sweet and fragrant. It is the dried leaf of a small evergreen shrub and has a pine flavor that is used not only in foods but in personal fragrances as well.

Salt *(Namak sambhar)*—Originally used as a preservative and less as a seasoning, salt's widespread use has led to medical research which indicates and demands reduced consumption. Prudent handling of salt in cooking is advised. Commercial sausages are heavily salted because of salt's preservative characteristics and because the public has developed a taste for its flavor. Government restriction may soon affect its use. Available in a fine grind and a coarse grind (kosher), salt can enhance and flavor but must never dominate.

Savory *(Satureja hortensis)*—Also called summer savory, this spice is another member of the mint family. Savory has a piquant flavor lending itself well to blending with other herbs and spices.

Sesame Seed *(Sesamum indicum)*—Used before the birth of Christ, this popular seed is cultivated in Central America, China, and India. Sesame's nutlike flavor changes somewhat if toasted and it imparts zest and crunchiness to products.

Tarragon *(Artemisia dracunculus)*—Imported here from France and also grown in the temperate zones of the United States, tarragon is very distinctive in flavor and is used extensively in haute cuisine in both fresh and dry forms. Tarragon is the green leaves of a perennial shrub and its taste is aromatic.

Thyme *(Thymus vulgaris)*—An enhancer in cooking and in liqueurs, thyme is cultivated extensively in France in many varieties, including lemon, and is also grown in the United States. A member of the mint family, it has a distinctive, pungent flavor and is widely used to flavor meat, fish, and poultry.

Turmeric *(Curcuma longa)*—Imported to the U.S. from Peru, Haiti, Jamaica, and India, turmeric is the root of a plant of the ginger family and has a slightly bitter taste. In Asia, turmeric has long played a part in religious and matrimonial rituals. Turmeric is an essential ingredient in curry powder blends and in prepared mustard.

SAUSAGE
MAKING
INSTRUCTIONS

Chapter 5

Cleanliness

The most important thing to remember about making sausage is that you will be using fresh meat, primarily pork, which you, your family, and your friends will be eating. As with any meal preparation, cleanliness should be the first priority. In dealing with ground meat it is *absolutely* essential.

Each cut into a piece of meat increases the number of surfaces which, if care is not exercised, will attract disease-causing bacteria. With ground meat used for sausage, or even as hamburgers, the danger increases dramatically because the number of surfaces increases dramatically.

Therefore, absolute attention to cleanliness and sanitation is mandatory and certain precautions must not be neglected.

The first step then in making sausage is to wash your hands and wrists thoroughly and dry them on a clean towel.

The same attention to cleanliness should then be focused on the equipment you are using. A wooden cutting board should be scrubbed, rinsed, and dried before placing meat on it. Take the same precautions with the knives, the scale, the grinder, and the stuffer you use.

Preparing the Casings

Sausage casings are usually sold in large bundles, one-pound cups, or by the yard. Most come in dry salted form.

The required lengths of casings should be removed from the salt container and rinsed thoroughly under cold running water. They should then be soaked in clear cold water for about thirty minutes before using.

Before stuffing, open one end of each length of casing to separate, then hold it under the faucet and let cold water run

Above: Sausage casings should be soaked for 30 minutes in a small bowl of cold water to remove the excess salt before stuffing them. Below: After the soaking period, casings are rinsed thoroughly with cold running water. (Photos by Bernadine M. Rechner)

through the entire length. After this rinsing, the casings are ready to stuff.

Leftover casings, which can be stored almost indefinitely, should be repacked in their original container and refrigerated until needed.

Preparing the Meat

The meat should be cold when it is trimmed of fat and cold when it is ground. A temperature of 30 to 32 degrees F. is ideal for these purposes and will deter bacterial growth. Ice cubes in the recipes are used for the same purpose.

For some coarse cut sausage, the meat is processed through the grinder once using the grinder plate with holes about $3/16$ inch in diameter.

Some fine-cut sausage takes two runs through the grinder. The first grinding should be through the cutting plate with holes about $3/8$ inch in diameter and the second through the plate with the smaller $3/16$ inch holes. The meat should be kept very cold between each grinding to prevent overheating. The grinder head should also be refrigerated between each grinding—there is no need to wash it between uses.

Grind the meat into a container large enough to allow hand mixing of the necessary spices into the meat. A container that is too small may cause spillage and poor distribution of the seasonings.

Once the meat and the spices are well blended, sauté a sample of the mixture until it is thoroughly cooked. Let the sample cool slightly and taste it carefully to determine if it is seasoned to your liking. If not, you can adjust the spices in the meat mixture, and then it is ready to stuff into the casings.

Stuffing the Casings

Following the manufacturer's instructions, attach the special sausage stuffer horn to your grinder after removing the cutting knife and plate. To elminate unnecessary air in the casings, push

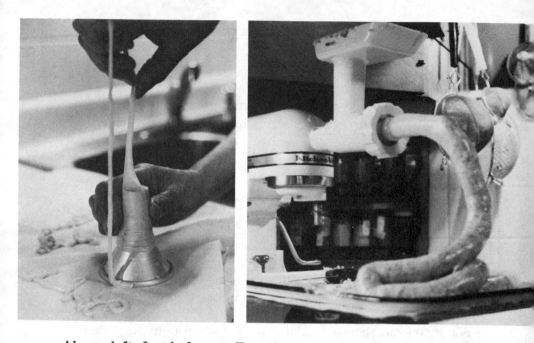

Above, left: Just before stuffing, the wet casings are slipped onto a hand stuffing funnel or the stuffer attachment of a meat grinder. Above, right: As the casing fills with sausage meat, it is eased off the end of the grinder's stuffer horn. Below: Gentle finger pressure pushes the sausage meat into the casings through a hand stuffing funnel. (Photos by Bernadine M. Rechner)

the ground sausage meat through the grinder into the stuffer horn until the meat reaches the tip. Slip the open end of the prepared casing length over the outside tip of the stuffer horn and work the entire length of the casing onto the tube until the end of the casing is about 1½ inches from the mouth of the tube. The casing will appear "bunched up" on the stuffer horn.

Hold the end of the casing in one hand and start the grinder on medium speed. At the same time, press the sausage mixture into the casing gently and evenly using the wooden pusher at the hopper end of the grinder. As the casing fills, gently ease it away from the tip of the horn.

Do not pack the meat into the casing too tightly; there must be enough room to permit twisting the sausage into links. If an air pocket develops in the casing, pierce it with a skewer or a needle.

When the last of the meat has been put into the grinder, add some stale bread or ice cubes and grind it up with the meat. The bread or ice will help get all the meat out of the grinder.

To twist the sausage into links, lay out the length of encased meat and twist it in the center. Then take lengths of sausage about two inches on either side of the center twist and twist one piece across the other. Continue twisting at about two-inch intervals down the length of the sausage.

You can also stuff sausage by hand with the help of a stuffing funnel. The funnel neck is inserted into the open end of the casings and the meat mixture is fed into the hopper end. Press the meat gently with your fingers through the funnel into the casings.

If you are planning to use the sausage meat in stuffings, stews, soups, skillet dinners, or casseroles or would like to make sausage patties or balls, it is not necessary to stuff the meat into casings. If the meat is tightly wrapped in plastic wrap it can be kept one or two days in the refrigerator or one month in a freezer set at zero degrees F. or below.

All sausage meat, whether loose or in casings, must be cooked thoroughly before serving.

SAUSAGE
RECIPES

Chapter 6

BACON SAUSAGE

The bacon added to the pork provides this sausage with a smoky taste that you will enjoy. This recipe is a good way to use bacon ends which you can purchase inexpensively at the supermarket delicatessen.

1¼ pounds pork shoulder
¾ pound bacon
3 ice cubes
1 teaspoon coarse salt
1 teaspoon sugar
1 teaspoon celery seed
1 teaspoon sweet paprika
½ teaspoon freshly ground
   black pepper

½ teaspoon ground
   coriander
¼ teaspoon ground ginger
1 tablespoon dehydrated
   minced onions
2 tablespoons water
50 inches natural pork
   casings
1 large egg white, unbeaten

Grind pork and bacon together using the small hole plate on grinder. Add ice cubes during grinding to keep meats cold and clear grinder. Add salt to ground meats; mix well. Refrigerate.

Mix sugar and all spices in a small bowl. Reconstitute onions in water in a second small bowl. Prepare casings according to instructions. (See Index.)

Add spice mixture, onions, and egg white to ground meats. Mix thoroughly.

Sauté a small amount of sausage in a lightly oiled frying pan until thoroughly cooked. Taste and adjust seasonings, if desired.

Stuff sausage into casings according to manufacturer's instructions that accompany grinder or use hand stuffing funnel. Do not overstuff.

To form links, place length of sausage on a flat surface and twist in center. Then begin twisting together links of desired size, one from each side of the center twist. Continue until all links are twisted. Refrigerate sausage uncovered several hours (at least 2).

To serve, sauté sausage slowly in a lightly oiled frying pan until brown and thoroughly cooked.

Makes 2 pounds.

BOUDIN BLANC

You would be hard pressed to find a shop where this heavenly sausage could be purchased. The pleasure you will have in eating Boudin Blanc will amply compensate for the time spent in its preparation.

1½ pounds center pork loin
12 ounces chicken breast
3 slices firm-textured bread such as homemade or French bread, crusts removed
½ cup light cream or half-and-half, scalded, cooled
3 eggs
1 egg white

2 teaspoons salt
1 teaspoon sugar
1 teaspoon freshly ground white pepper
½ teaspoon mace
½ teaspoon freshly ground nutmeg
50 inches natural pork casings
1 teaspoon sugar

In the food processor, using steel knife, process meats. (This should be done in two batches.) Reserve.

Soak bread in cream. Beat eggs and egg white in a small bowl until mixed. Mix salt, 1 teaspoon sugar, and spices in a second small bowl. Add soaked bread, eggs, and spice mixture to batches of processed meats. Cover and refrigerate at least several hours.

Prepare casings according to instructions. (See Index.) Sauté a small amount of boudin in a lightly buttered frying pan. Taste and adjust seasonings, if desired. Stuff sausage into casings according to manufacturer's instructions that accompany grinder or use hand stuffing funnel. This is an emulsion and requires patience when stuffing the casings. Do not overstuff.

To form links, place length of boudin on a flat surface and twist in center. Then begin twisting together two-inch lengths, one from each side at the center twist. Continue until all links are twisted.

Heat a large saucepan or Dutch oven of water, to which 1 teaspoon sugar has been added, to boiling. Reduce heat. Place sausages in a fry basket or colander and immerse in water. Do not boil. Poach sausage gently for about 5 minutes. Drain and dry. Refrigerate uncovered for several hours (at least 2).

To serve, sauté sausage slowly in a lightly buttered frying pan until thoroughly cooked. Sausage can be refrigerated for 2 or 3 days or frozen for longer periods.

Note: If food processor is not available, grind meats twice using small hole plate on grinder; then beat with a mixer after adding spices. This sausage should form a pastelike texture.

Makes 2½ pounds.

BRATWURST

All our tasters loved this Bratwurst and you will, too. It's wonderful served on a roll like a "hot dog."

½ pound beef
1½ pounds pork
½ pound pork fat
4 ice cubes
1 tablespoon coarse salt
1 teaspoon freshly ground
    black pepper
1 teaspoon ground
    coriander
½ teaspoon dry mustard
½ teaspoon sweet paprika
¼ teaspoon mace
About 50 inches natural
    pork casings

Grind beef using the large hole plate on grinder. Grind pork and pork fat together using the small hole plate on grinder.

Combine ground meats. Add ice cubes during grinding to keep meats cold and clear grinder. Add salt; mix well. Mix spices in a small bowl. Add to ground meats. Mix thoroughly. Refrigerate.

Prepare casings according to instructions. (See Index.)

Stuff sausage into casings according to manufacturer's instructions that accompany grinder or use hand stuffing funnel. Refrigerate sausage uncovered several hours. Turn sausages over; refrigerate at least several more hours, to enhance the flavor of the Bratwurst.

To serve, sauté sausage slowly in a lightly oiled frying pan until brown and thoroughly cooked.

Makes 2½ pounds.

BREAKFAST BEEF SAUSAGE

This tasty sausage will be a welcome change from pork sausage or for those whose diet restricts pork. You'll make it often—for breakfast, lunch, or dinner.

1½ pounds beef chuck
½ pounds beef fat
2 ice cubes
2 teaspoons coarse salt
1 teaspoon sugar
1 teaspoon sage
1 teaspoon freshly ground
    black pepper
½ teaspoon ground red
    pepper
½ teaspoon summer savory
¼ teaspoon celery seed
¼ teaspoon ground nutmeg
¼ teaspoon powdered
    thyme
50 inches natural pork casings

Grind meat and fat together using the large hole plate on grinder. Add ice cubes during grinding to keep meat cold and clear grinder. Add salt; mix well. Refrigerate covered several hours. Refrigerate grinder head.

Mix sugar, spices, and herbs in a small bowl. Add to ground beef; mix thoroughly. Regrind mixture using the small hole plate on grinder.

Sauté a small amount of sausage in lightly oiled frying pan.

Sausage does not need to be thoroughly cooked as meat can be eaten rare. Taste and adjust seasonings, if desired.

Prepare casings according to instructions. (See Index.)

Stuff sausage into casings according to manufacturer's instructions that accompany grinder or use hand stuffing funnel. Sausage can also be made in a country roll as follows. Place two 12-inch pieces of plastic wrap on a flat surface. Divide sausage in half. Place each half on a piece of plastic wrap. Wrap sausage and twist ends tightly to compact. Refrigerate at least 12 hours. To serve, slice sausage; sauté in a lightly oiled frying pan. Do not overcook as sausage does not have to be brown throughout.

Sausage can be refrigerated for several days or frozen for longer periods.

Makes 2 pounds.

BROWN 'N' SERVE SAUSAGE

The following recipe makes a savory sausage that is free of additives, convenient for those who like a quick breakfast or snack, and it freezes well.

1½ pounds ground pork loin
½ pound pork fat
3 ice cubes
2 teaspoons salt
2 teaspoons sugar

1 teaspoon ground black
  pepper
1 teaspoon sage
¼ teaspoon ground nutmeg
¼ teaspoon ground ginger
1 egg white, unbeaten

Grind pork and pork fat together using the small hole plate on grinder. Add ice cubes during grinding to keep meat cold and clear grinder. Mix salt, sugar, and spices in a small bowl. Add egg white and spice mixture to ground pork; mix thoroughly. Cover and refrigerate for several hours (at least 2), until very cold.

Sauté a small amount of sausage in a lightly oiled frying pan until thoroughly cooked. Taste and adjust seasonings, if desired.

Run cold sausage through stuffer with no casings. Cut off desired length. Heat a large saucepan or Dutch oven of water to boiling. Place sausage in a fry basket or colander and immerse in boiling water. Reduce heat; simmer sausage several minutes. Remove sausage when it floats to the surface of water. Drain sausage on a rack; cool. Refrigerate sausage covered for at least 2 hours.

Sausage can be refrigerated for several days or frozen for longer periods.

To serve, sauté sausage in a lightly oiled frying pan until brown but not dry. Do not overcook.

Makes 2 pounds.

CHILI SAUSAGE

You will enjoy the piquant flavor of this sausage and the novel way you can serve it.

2 pounds beef chuck,
    including 25 percent fat
2 ice cubes
2 teaspoons coarse salt
1 teaspoon sugar
3 to 4 teaspoons chili powder
1 teaspoon coarsely ground
    black pepper
1 teaspoon cumin

½ teaspoon dry mustard
½ teaspoon crushed red
    pepper (or use ancho or
    pasilla from a Mexican
    food store)
2 teaspoons dehydrated
    minced onions
3 tablespoons water

Grind beef chuck using the large hole plate on grinder. Run 1 ice cube through grinder. Add salt to ground beef. Mix sugar and spices in a small bowl. Reconstitute onions in water. Add spice mixture and onions to ground beef; mix thoroughly. Regrind meat mixture using the large hole plate on grinder. Run second ice cube through grinder. Refrigerate sausage several hours.

Place a 14-inch piece of plastic wrap on a flat surface. Shape sausage into a 3-inch roll. Place sausage on plastic wrap. Wrap sausage and twist ends tightly. Roll the cylinder several times until compact. Sausage can be refrigerated 2 to 3 days or frozen no longer than 1 month.

For serving suggestion, see recipe for Tacos in index.

Note: It is not necessary to wash grinder between grindings but it is absolutely essential to place grinder in refrigerator to avoid bacteria buildup.

Makes about 2 pounds.

CHORIZOS

If it is a hot, spicy sausage you enjoy, this Mexican variety will suit your tastes. The spices can be reduced for those preferring a milder flavor.

1½ pounds pork
½ pound pork fat
2 teaspoons coarse salt
4 to 6 dried chili peppers
4 cloves garlic
2 tablespoons water
1 teaspoon sugar
2 teaspoons sweet paprika
1 teaspoon chili powder
1 teaspoon crushed red
  pepper
1 teaspoon ground coriander

1 teaspoon cumin
½ teaspoon coriander seed,
  crushed
½ teaspoon dry mustard
¼ teaspoon ground
  cinnamon
¼ teaspoon oregano
⅓ cup distilled white
  vinegar
⅓ cup cracker crumbs
60 inches natural pork
  casings

Grind pork and fat together using the large hole plate on grinder. Add salt to ground pork; mix well. Refrigerate.

Prepare casings according to instructions. (See Index.)

Process chili peppers, including seeds, in a blender. Add garlic and water; blend until a paste is formed. Reserve.

Mix sugar and spices in a small bowl. Add chili paste, spice mixture, and vinegar to ground pork; mix thoroughly. Add cracker crumbs; mix again. Refrigerate meat mixture covered until chilled, about 30 minutes.

Stuff sausage into casings according to manufacturer's instructions that accompany grinder or use hand stuffing funnel. Do not overstuff. Refrigerate sausage uncovered several hours, turning once during that period.

To serve, saute sausage gently in a lightly oiled frying pan until brown and thoroughly cooked. Serve hot, wrapped around a warm tortilla shell, or in any recipe calling for chorizo.

Makes 2¼ pounds.

CITY CHICKEN SAUSAGE

Anyone who has ever savored city chicken—pieces of pork and veal on a skewer—will love this delicate-flavored sausage.

1 pound pork shoulder
1 pound veal breast
2 teaspoons coarse salt
½ teaspoon ground black pepper
½ teaspoon freshly grated nutmeg
1 tablespoon unflavored gelatin softened in 1 tablespoon cold water, then dissolved over warm water with an additional tablespoon of water

2 eggs, beaten
2 tablespoons water
¼ teaspoon salt
About ¼ cup instant flour (such as Wondra®)
About ½ cup fine dry bread crumbs
¼ cup vegetable oil
Wooden skewers

Grind pork and veal using coarse plate on grinder. Immediately regrind using the small hole plate on grinder. Add salt and remaining spices. Prepare gelatin, cool slightly and add to mixture, kneading meats while pouring gelatin. Refrigerate several hours.

Shape meat into walnut-size balls (about 30 to a pound). Place 5 to 6 sausage balls to a wooden skewer. Continue until all meat is skewered.

To cook and serve: Mix eggs, 2 tablespoons water, and ¼ teaspoon salt in a large bowl. Place instant flour on a piece of wax paper. Place bread crumbs on a second sheet of wax paper. Roll skewered sausage first in flour, then in egg mixture and then in bread crumbs, making the crumbs completely coat meat. (Add more flour and bread crumbs to wax paper if necessary.) Refrigerate sausage uncovered for at least 1 hour.

Preheat oven to 425°. Place vegetable oil on a four-sided baking sheet; heat baking sheet in oven until hot. Carefully remove from oven; roll skewered sausage in oil to coat using tongs to avoid burns. When all have been completed, lay sausage on baking sheet. Bake sausage for 15 minutes. Serve immediately with potato or macaroni and vegetable.

Note: Wooden skewers may be obtained from your butcher when purchasing meat.

Makes 2 pounds.

CLUB SAUSAGE

You have eaten club sandwiches made with chicken, ham, and cheese. Now try the combination in a sausage!

3 slices firm-textured
    bread, crusts removed
½ cup cold water
⅛ cup instant nonfat dry milk
2 cups cooked chicken
2 cups cooked ham
1 cup finely diced Gruyère
    cheese
1 teaspoon salt
1 teaspoon freshly ground
    white pepper

½ teaspoon ground nutmeg
3 tablespoons finely minced
    fresh parsley
1 tablespoon finely minced
    fresh chives or 1
    tablespoon finely
    minced green onion tops
½ teaspoon dry mustard
50 inches natural pork
    casings

Crumble bread into a small bowl. Add water and dry milk. Let bread soak until liquid is absorbed.

Grind chicken and ham using the large hole plate on grinder. Add bread mixture and cheese to ground meats. Add remaining ingredients except casings; mix well. Refrigerate.

Prepare casings according to instructions. (See Index.) Stuff sausage into casings according to instructions that accompany grinder or use hand stuffing funnel. It is important that casings be stuffed loosely to allow for expansion and melting of cheese. To form links, place length of sausage on a flat surface and twist in center. Then begin twisting together 2-inch lengths, one from each side of the center twist. Continue until all links are twisted. Refrigerate sausage several hours.

To serve, simmer sausage in water in a deep frying pan until heated. (Since all ingredients are cooked, it is necessary only to heat sausage.) Do not boil or casings will burst. Serve sausage on a roll for a luncheon meal.

Makes 1½ pounds.

CURRY SAUSAGE

This spicy sausage is excellent for dinner served with steamed rice.

¼ cup shredded coconut
¼ cup apple juice
1½ pounds pork shoulder
½ pound pork fat
2 teaspoons coarse salt
2 tablespoons dehydrated minced onions
2 tablespoons water
2 tablespoons hot curry powder
1 teaspoon mild curry powder
1 clove garlic, finely minced or pressed
50 inches natural pork casings

Soak coconut in apple juice in small bowl for about 30 minutes.

Grind pork and pork fat together using the large hole plate on grinder. Regrind. Add salt to ground pork; mix thoroughly. Reconstitute onions in water in a small bowl. Mix curry powders. Add onions, curries, and garlic to ground pork. Strain coconut; pour apple juice into ground pork. Mix well. Refrigerate mixture 2 hours.

Prepare casings according to instructions. (See Index.)

Sauté a small amount of sausage in a lightly oiled frying pan until thoroughly cooked. Taste and adjust seasonings, if desired.

Fill casings with sausage mixture using a hand stuffing funnel. Refrigerate uncovered several hours (at least 2), turning sausage once during that period. Sausage can be refrigerated 2 to 3 days, or frozen for longer periods.

To serve, sauté sausage gently in a lightly oiled frying pan until brown and thoroughly cooked.

Makes about 2 pounds.

DIET SAUSAGE

We developed this recipe for those who like sausage but are restricted in their salt and fat intake. No salt is called for here, and by grinding your own meat, you can control the fat content. Properly cooked, this sausage will be appealing and enjoyable.

1 pound lean pork
1 pound beef chuck,
   trimmed of visible fat
1 tablespoon dehydrated
   minced onions
2 tablespoons cold water
1 teaspoon sugar
1 teaspoon sage

1 teaspoon freshly ground
   black pepper
½ teaspoon ground red
   pepper
½ teaspoon sweet paprika
½ teaspoon ground nutmeg
About 50 inches natural
   pork casings

Grind pork and beef together using the large hole plate on grinder. Regrind using the small hole plate on grinder.

Reconstitute onions in cold water. Mix sugar and spices in a small bowl. Add onions and spice mixture to ground meats; mix thoroughly. Refrigerate.

Prepare casings according to instructions. (See Index.) Sauté a small amount of sausage in a lightly oiled frying pan until thoroughly cooked. Taste and adjust seasonings, if desired. Stuff sausage into casings according to instructions that accompany grinder or use hand stuffing funnel.

To form links, place length of sausage on a flat surface. Twist in center. Then begin twisting together 2-inch lengths, one from each side of the center twist. Continue until all links are twisted. Refrigerate sausage uncovered at least 12 hours.

To serve, poach sausage gently in tomato sauce, vegetable juice, or beef stock until thoroughly cooked. This method will add flavor and keep sausage from tasting dry.

Makes 2 pounds.

ELK SAUSAGE

The elk meat for this delicious sausage was supplied by Bob Schoedler of Colorado. The recipe can also be made with venison, which may be more readily available. This sausage is great to smoke if you have the facilities.

1½ pounds elk meat
¼ cup vegetable oil
½ pound pork shoulder or pork loin ends
½ pound pork fat
3 ice cubes
½ cup finely minced onion
2 cloves garlic, finely minced or pressed

1 tablespoon brown sugar
4 teaspoons coarse salt
2 teaspoons Juniper berries, crushed
Grated rind of 1 lemon
1 tablespoon lemon juice
¼ cup dry white wine
50 inches natural pork casings

Dice elk meat; pour vegetable oil over meat in a large bowl. Stir to coat the meat evenly. Cover and refrigerate at least several hours or overnight.

Grind elk, pork, and pork fat together using the large hole plate on grinder. Regrind. Add ice cubes during grinding to keep meats cold and clear grinder. Add remaining ingredients, except casings, to ground meats; mix thoroughly. Cover and refrigerate.

Prepare casings according to instructions. (See Index.)

Sauté a small amount of sausage in a lightly oiled frying pan until thoroughly cooked. Taste and adjust seasonings, if desired. Stuff sausage into casings according to manufacturer's instructions that accompany grinder or use hand stuffing funnel.

To form links, place length of sausage on a flat surface. Twist in center. Then begin twisting together 2-inch lengths, one from each side of the center twist. Continue until all links are twisted. Refrigerate uncovered for several hours, turning once during that period. Sausage can be refrigerated for several days or frozen for longer periods.

To serve, poach sausage gently in water to cover in a frying pan for 5 minutes. Drain and dry. Sauté sausage in a lightly oiled frying pan until brown and thoroughly cooked.

Makes 2¼ pounds.

FAVORITE BREAKFAST SAUSAGE

Bertie's family has enjoyed this recipe for years, as have many of the students whom she has taught in her adult high school education program. This sausage will become a staple at your house, too.

1½ pounds ground pork
½ pound ground pork fat
2 ice cubes
2 teaspoons salt
½ teaspoon sage
½ teaspoon ground black
    pepper
¼ teaspoon sugar

⅛ teaspoon ground red
    pepper
⅛ teaspoon sweet paprika
⅛ teaspoon celery seed
Dash ground ginger
Dash ground nutmeg

Grind pork and pork fat together using the small hole plate on grinder. Add ice cubes during grinding to keep meat cold and clear grinder. Mix remaining ingredients in a small bowl; add to ground pork. Mix thoroughly. Refrigerate for 2 hours.

Sauté a small amount of sausage in a lightly oiled frying pan until thoroughly cooked. Taste and adjust seasonings, if desired.

Place two 12-inch pieces of plastic wrap on a flat surface. Place half the sausage on each piece. Wrap sausage and twist ends tightly. Roll sausage several times to compact meat. Refrigerate sausage at least overnight.

To serve, slice sausage rolls. Sauté slices in a lightly oiled frying pan until thoroughly cooked. Serve with pancakes or eggs, or in a sandwich.

Makes 2 pounds.

FRESH HERB SAUSAGE

This delectable sausage is for those wise enough to have an herb garden. Unfortunately, it can only be enjoyed in the growing season unless you are successful with window box herbs. Most herb combinations will make a good sausage so long as they include sage.

2 pounds pork, cut from
    loin end
20 stems chives
8 to 10 large basil leaves
6 to 8 sage leaves
8 stems of thyme, leaves
    only
8 stems of marjoram, leaves
    only
8 stems of oregano, leaves
    only
6 stems of summer savory,
    leaves only

6 stems of parsley, flat type
    leaf preferable, leaves
    only
2 ice cubes
2 teaspoons coarse salt
2 teaspoons freshly ground
    white pepper
2 teaspoons sugar
2 tablespoons unbeaten egg
    white
50 inches natural pork
    casings

Grind pork and herbs together using the large hole plate on grinder. Add ice cubes during grinding to keep meat cold and clear grinder. Add remaining ingredients except casings. Mix thoroughly. Regrind mixture using the small hole plate on grinder. Refrigerate covered at least 12 hours or overnight.

Prepare casings according to instructions. (See Index.) Stuff sausage into casings according to manufacturer's instructions that accompany grinder or use hand stuffing funnel. Do not overstuff.

To form links, place length of sausage on a flat surface. Twist in center. Then begin twisting together 2-inch lengths, one from each side of the center twist. Continue until all links are twisted. Refrigerate sausage uncovered several hours (at least 2) before serving. Sausage can be refrigerated several days or frozen for longer periods.

To serve, sauté sausage gently in a lightly oiled frying pan until brown and thoroughly cooked. Serve with freshly made pasta.

Makes 2 pounds.

GREEK SAUSAGE

If you have never had the pleasure of eating Greek sausage, make some soon. The orange zest imparts a unique flavor that you will enjoy.

1½ pounds pork meat
2 ice cubes
¼ pound pork fat
2 teaspoons coarse salt
½ teaspoon sugar
½ teaspoon cumin
½ teaspoon ground black
　　pepper
¼ teaspoon ground
　　cinnamon
¼ teaspoon ground nutmeg
⅛ teaspoon ground allspice
2 to 3 tablespoons grated
　　fresh orange rind, all
　　white pith removed
½ cup dry rosé wine
50 inches natural pork
　　casings

Grind pork using the large hole plate on grinder. Run 1 ice cube through grinder. Grind fat using the small hole plate on grinder. Run second ice cube through grinder. Mix pork and pork fat. Mix salt, sugar, and spices in a small bowl. Add spice mixture, orange rind, and wine to ground pork; mix thoroughly. Refrigerate for about 1 hour.

Prepare casings according to directions. (See Index.)

Sauté a small amount of sausage in a lightly oiled frying pan until thoroughly cooked. Taste and adjust seasonings, if desired. Stuff sausage into casings according to manufacturer's instructions that accompany grinder or use hand stuffing funnel. Sausage can be refrigerated for 2 to 3 days or frozen for longer periods.

To serve, sauté sausage slowly in a lightly oiled frying pan until brown and thoroughly cooked.

Makes 2 pounds.

GYRO MEAT

Once you have tasted this delicious gyro meat, you will no longer buy it at a store. The meat is fun to make and very economical compared to the commercial variety. Increase or decrease seasoning for your personal taste.

1½ pounds shoulder lamb,
    including some fat
1 pound beef chuck,
    including some fat
¼ cup dehydrated minced
    onions
⅓ cup water
1 tablespoon salt
1 teaspoon sugar
2 teaspoons Greek oregano
2 teaspoons freshly ground
    coarse black pepper

1 teaspoon cumin
1 teaspoon hot paprika
½ teaspoon ground
    cinnamon
2 large cloves garlic, finely
    minced or pressed
2 tablespoons vegetable oil
8 slices blanched bacon or
    fresh pork belly, if
    available

Grind lamb and beef together using the large hole plate on grinder. Regrind using the small hole plate on grinder.

Reconstitute onions in water in a small bowl. Mix salt, sugar, and spices in a small bowl, blending well. Add onions, spice mixture, garlic, and oil to ground meats; mix thoroughly. Cover and refrigerate several hours (at least 2).

Sauté a small amount of gyro meat gently in a lightly oiled frying pan. (Meat need not be cooked long as both meats may be eaten rare.) Taste and adjust seasonings, if desired.

Blanch bacon by simmering in hot water about 3 minutes, drain and dry on paper towels.

Heat oven to 375°. Line a bread loaf pan, 8½ × 5 × 3 inches, with half the blanched bacon, covering sides and bottom. Pack gyro meat into bacon-lined pan, filling to top of pan. Cover meat with remaining bacon.

Place filled loaf pan in a larger pan of water, so water level reaches about three-fourths of the way up the sides of the loaf pan. Place both pans in oven; bake meat for about 20 minutes. Reduce heat to 350°; bake 30 minutes longer.

Remove pans from oven; remove loaf pan from water bath. Place loaf pan on a rack to cool. Cover with aluminum foil and a baking sheet on which a weight has been placed to compress the loaf. Cool.

Refrigerate meat covered with weight for 12 hours or overnight to ripen and increase flavor. Meat can be refrigerated several days.

Serve meat cold, thinly sliced. See also serving suggestion for Gyro sandwich recipe. (See Index.)

Makes 2 pounds.

HAM SAUSAGE

Savory ham—use your leftovers here—gives this sausage a slightly smoky taste, which we know you will like.

½ pound baked ham
1 pound pork shoulder
¼ pound ham fat or a
    combination of ham
    and pork fat
3 ice cubes
1 teaspoon salt
½ teaspoon sugar
1 teaspoon dry mustard

1 teaspoon ground black
    pepper
½ teaspoon sage
½ teaspoon ground nutmeg
½ teaspoon ground red
    pepper
¼ teaspoon celery seed
About 50 inches natural
    pork casings

Grind ham using the large hole plate on grinder. Grind pork and fat together using the small hole plate on grinder. Add ice cubes during grinding to keep meats cold and clear grinder. Mix ground meats. Add salt to mixture; refrigerate.

Mix sugar and spices in a small bowl. Add to meat mixture; mix thoroughly. Refrigerate meat mixture and grinder head.

Sauté a small amount of sausage in a lightly oiled frying pan until thoroughly cooked. Taste and adjust seasonings, if desired.

Prepare casings according to instructions. (See Index.)

Stuff sausage into casings according to manufacturer's instructions that accompany grinder, or use hand stuffing funnel.

To serve, sausage can be sautéed, baked, or broiled until thoroughly cooked. Use sausage in any casserole of your choice. This sausage will have a pink appearance even when cooked because of the ham content. Do not overcook.

Makes 1¾ pounds.

HERDER SAUSAGE

This lamb sausage will lend variety to your menu. Use it in casseroles or serve it on rolls for sandwich meals—no condiments needed.

2 pounds lamb, including
small amount of fat
2 ice cubes
2 teaspoons dehydrated
minced onions
2 tablespoons water
2 teaspoons very finely
minced fresh
gingerroot or ½
teaspoon ground ginger
1½ teaspoons tomato paste

2 teaspoons coarse salt
1 teaspoon sugar
1 teaspoon cumin
1 teaspoon ground
coriander
1 teaspoon coriander leaves,
crumbled
1 teaspoon turmeric
¾ teaspoon ground red
pepper

Grind lamb using the large hole plate on grinder. Add ice cubes during grinding to keep meat cold and clear grinder.

Reconstitute onions in water in a small bowl. Add gingerroot and tomato paste; mix well. Mix salt, sugar, and spices in a small bowl. Add onion mixture and spice mixture to ground lamb; mix thoroughly. Refrigerate 1 or 2 hours.

Sauté a small amount of sausage in a lightly oiled frying pan. Taste and adjust seasonings, if desired.

Place two 12-inch pieces of plastic wrap on a flat surface. Place half the sausage on each piece. Wrap sausage and twist ends tightly. Roll sausage to compact meat. Sausage can be refrigerated for 1 or 2 days or frozen for longer periods.

To serve, slice sausage. Sauté in a lightly oiled frying pan. (It is not necessary to cook for a long period, as lamb is best served medium rare.) Sausage can be used in any casserole dish or be served with rice and vegetables for dinner.

Makes about 2 pounds.

HOT ITALIAN SAUSAGE

For everyone who enjoys Italian sausage on the hot, spicy side, this recipe is ideal. We suggest you hand stuff this sausage so the meat will remain coarse.

1½ pounds pork shoulder
½ pound pork fat
Ice cubes
2 teaspoons coarse salt
1 tablespoon crushed red
   pepper
1 teaspoon coarsely ground
   black pepper

1 teaspoon ground red
   pepper
1 teaspoon hot paprika
½ to 1 teaspoon fennel seed,
   crushed
½ teaspoon sugar
50 to 60 inches natural
   pork casings

Grind pork and pork fat together using the large hole plate on grinder. Add 1 or 2 ice cubes during grinding to keep meat cold and clear grinder. Add 1 ice cube after all the meat has been ground (this will provide moisture for the seasonings).

Mix salt, spices, and sugar in a small bowl. Add spice mixture to ground meat; mix thoroughly. Cover and refrigerate for about 1 hour.

Prepare casings according to instructions. (See Index.)

Sauté a small amount of sausage in a lightly oiled frying pan until thoroughly cooked. Taste and adjust seasonings, if desired.

Stuff sausage into casings using a hand stuffing funnel. If this sausage will be used for pizza, leave as loose meat.

To serve, poach sausage gently in water to cover in a frying pan, about 10 minutes. Drain and dry. Sauté sausage slowly in a lightly oiled frying pan until brown and thoroughly cooked.

Makes 2 pounds.

HOT ITALIAN SAUSAGE—NO SEED

The following recipe is intended for those who like hot Italian sausage, but who do not enjoy the taste of fennel. Extra spices compensate for the loss of fennel taste. This is a good sausage for anyone who likes variety, too.

1½ pounds pork shoulder
½ pound pork fat
2 ice cubes
2 teaspoons coarse salt
1 tablespoon crushed red
  pepper
2 teaspoons coarsely ground
  black pepper

1 teaspoon ground red
  pepper
1 teaspoon hot paprika
1 teaspoon sugar
50 inches natural pork
  casings

Grind pork and pork fat together using the large hole plate on grinder. Add ice cubes during grinding to keep meat cold and clear grinder.

Mix salt, spices, and sugar in a small bowl. Add to ground meat; mix thoroughly. Cover and refrigerate several hours (at least 2).

Sauté a small amount of sausage in a lightly oiled frying pan until thoroughly cooked. Taste and adjust seasonings, if desired.

Prepare casings according to instructions. (See Index.)

To retain the coarse texture of the meat, stuff sausage into casings using hand stuffing funnel. If the sausage will be used on pizza or as a base for spaghetti sauce, leave as loose meat.

Sausage can be refrigerated for 2 to 3 days or frozen for longer periods.

To serve, bake, broil, or sauté sausage until brown and thoroughly cooked.

Makes 2 pounds.

ITALIAN PEASANT SAUSAGE

The pork rind in this sausage provides a different texture which is most pleasing to the palate.

½ pound pork rind (if unavailable, use pork hocks)
1½ pounds pork shoulder
2 teaspoons coarse salt
1 teaspoon sugar
1 teaspoon coarsely ground black pepper

1 teaspoon oregano leaves, finely crumbled
½ teaspoon powdered bay leaf
½ teaspoon sage
½ teaspoon hot paprika or ground red pepper
50 inches natural pork casings

Cook pork rind or hocks in water to cover until tender, but not soft. (A small onion, bay leaf, and some parsley added to the water will make the meat tastier). Remove meat and cool. Reserve stock.

Grind pork and pork rind together, using the small hole plate on grinder. Regrind to make a fine-textured sausage. Add salt, sugar, and spices to ground meats; mix thoroughly. Refrigerate for about 1 hour.

Prepare casings according to instructions. (See Index.)

Sauté a small amount of sausage in a lightly oiled frying pan until thoroughly cooked. Taste and adjust the seasonings, if desired.

Stuff sausage into casings according to manufacturer's instructions that accompany grinder or use hand stuffing funnel. Refrigerate until serving time.

Sausage can be refrigerated 2 to 3 days or frozen for longer periods. Sausage can be used in any recipe calling for Italian sausage. The reserved stock and the meat from the hocks can be used for a delicious bean soup.

Makes 2 pounds.

ITALIAN SAUSAGE WITH WINE AND HERBS

If you like Italian sausage you will especially enjoy the unusual taste of this one. It is delicious served with polenta.

1½ pounds pork
¾ pound beef chuck
¼ pound pork fat
2 ice cubes
2 teaspoons salt
1 teaspoon coarsely ground
    black pepper
½ teaspoon crushed red
    pepper

½ cup finely chopped fresh
    parsley
⅓ cup grated Parmesan or
    Romano cheese
10 fresh basil leaves,
    minced, or ½ teaspoon
    dry basil leaves
½ cup dry red wine
About 60 inches natural
    pork casings

Grind pork, beef, and fat together twice using the large hole plate on grinder. Add ice cubes during grinding to keep meats cold and clear grinder. Add salt to ground meats; mix thoroughly. Mix peppers, parsley, cheese, and basil in a small bowl. Add to meat mixture. Add wine to mixture; mix thoroughly. Refrigerate.

Prepare casings according to instructions. (See Index.)

Sauté a small amount of sausage in a lightly oiled frying pan until thoroughly cooked. Taste and adjust seasonings, if desired.

Stuff sausage into casings according to manufacturer's instructions that accompany grinder or use hand stuffing funnel. Refrigerate sausage until serving time. Sausage can be refrigerated for 2 to 3 days or frozen for longer periods.

Use sausage in recipe for Polenta or recipe for Sausage Spaghetti Sauce. (See Index for both recipes.) Sausage can also be simply sautéed in a lightly oiled frying pan until brown and thoroughly cooked and served as a dinner item.

Makes 2½ pounds.

KEBBEE

For a different, interesting meal, be sure to try this tasty sausage. It is nutritious, too, with its cracked wheat!

1 cup fine cracked bulgur
    (cracked wheat)
2 cups water
2 pounds ground lamb
    shoulder, including ½
    pound fat
⅓ cup dehydrated minced
    onions
⅓ cup water
2 tablespoons coarse salt

2 teaspoons freshly ground
    black pepper
1 teaspoon ground allspice
1 teaspoon sugar
1 teaspoon summer savory
¼ teaspoon ground cloves
2 large cloves garlic,
    finely minced or
    pressed
60 inches natural pork casings

Soak bulgur in 2 cups water for about 1 or 1½ hours or until bulgur is thoroughly swollen. Drain bulgur; squeeze out excess water. Add to ground lamb. Reconstitute onions in ⅓ cup water in a small bowl. Add onions and salt to lamb mixture. Mix thoroughly. Refrigerate.

Mix remaining ingredients, except casings, in a small bowl.

Prepare casings according to instructions. (See Index.) Add spice mixture to lamb mixture; mix thoroughly. Sauté a small amount of sausage in a lightly oiled frying pan. Taste and adjust seasonings, if desired.

Stuff sausage into casings according to manufacturer's instructions that accompany grinder or use hand stuffing funnel. Refrigerate sausage uncovered for several hours before serving, turning once during that period. Sausage can be refrigerated, covered, for several days, or frozen.

To serve, sauté sausage in a lightly oiled frying pan until brown. (It is not necessary to thoroughly cook meat as in pork sausages. Lamb should be eaten underdone for best flavor.)

Makes 2¼ pounds.

KIELBASA

You have surely missed one of the "stars" among sausages, if you have never eaten Polish sausage. Do try our version approved by friends who understand Polish sausage.

1 pound pork shoulder
½ pound beef chuck
½ pound pork fat
2 ice cubes
2 teaspoons coarse salt
½ teaspoon sugar
1 teaspoon coarsely ground
    black pepper

1 teaspoon ground
    marjoram
¼ teaspoon ground nutmeg
⅛ teaspoon ground allspice
4 cloves garlic, finely
    minced or pressed
50 inches natural pork
    casings

Grind pork, beef, and pork fat together using the large hole plate on grinder. Add ice cubes during grinding to keep meats cold and clear grinder.

Mix salt, sugar, ground spices, and garlic in a small bowl; mix well. Add to meat mixture. Mix thoroughly. Refrigerate for at least 2 hours.

Sauté a small amount of sausage in a lightly oiled frying pan until thoroughly cooked. Taste and adjust seasonings, if desired.

Prepare casings according to instructions. (See Index.)

Stuff sausage into casings according to manufacturer's instructions that accompany grinder or use hand stuffing funnel. Refrigerate sausage uncovered, several hours, turning sausage once after 2 to 3 hours.

To serve, simmer sausage in water to cover about 10 minutes. Drain and dry. Sauté sausage in a lightly oiled frying pan until brown and thoroughly cooked.

Makes 2 pounds.

KRAUT SAUSAGE

This is the sausage for those who like pork in combination with a subtle taste of sauerkraut and a hint of potato flavor.

2 tablespoons dehydrated
　potato flakes
4 teaspoons coarse salt
1½ teaspoons caraway seeds
1½ teaspoons hot paprika
1½ teaspoons coarsely
　ground black pepper
1 teaspoon ground coriander
1 teaspoon sugar
½ teaspoon thyme
1 tablespoon dehydrated
　onions

2 tablespoons cold water
6 juniper berries, crushed
2 pounds pork shoulder or
　pork loin ends
10 ounces pork fat
10 ounces sauerkraut,
　washed, drained,
　squeezed of water
2 ice cubes
60 inches natural pork
　casings

Mix potato flakes, salt, caraway, paprika, pepper, coriander, sugar, and thyme in a small bowl. Reconstitute onions in cold water in a second small bowl. Add juniper berries to onions.

Grind pork and pork fat together using the large hole plate on grinder. Add sauerkraut, onion-juniper berry mixture to grinder. Add ice to keep the meat cold and clear grinder. Add spice mixture to meat mixture; mix thoroughly. Refrigerate sausage covered at least several hours.

Prepare casings according to instructions. (See Index.) Sauté a small amount of sausage in a lightly oiled frying pan until thoroughly cooked. Taste and adjust seasonings, if desired.

Stuff sausage into casings according to manufacturer's instructions that accompany grinder or use hand stuffing funnel. Do not overstuff. To form links, lay out length of sausage on a flat surface and twist in center. Then begin twisting together 2-inch lengths, one from each side of the center twist. Continue until all links are twisted.

Refrigerate sausage uncovered for several hours (at least 2), turning sausage once during that period.

To serve, simmer sausage in water to cover for 5 minutes. Do not boil. Drain well. Sauté sausage slowly in a lightly oiled frying pan until brown and thoroughly cooked. Serve hot.

Makes 2¾ pounds.

LAMB BURGERS

A welcome change from a hamburger is a lamb burger—easily made from ground lamb breast or lamb shoulder. Lamb burgers are seasoned with mint and cooked only until medium rare.

2 pounds ground lamb,
    including some fat
1 cup finely minced onions
2 teaspoons coarse salt
¼ cup finely minced fresh
    parsley
1 tablespoon fresh mint,
    finely chopped, or 1
    teaspoon dry mint
    flakes

1 teaspoon freshly ground
    black pepper
½ teaspoon marjoram
½ teaspoon ground allspice
1 teaspoon sugar
1 egg white, unbeaten

Combine ground lamb, onions, and salt; mix thoroughly. Mix spices and sugar in a small bowl; add to lamb mixture. Add egg white; mix thoroughly. Shape mixture into 3-inch patties and place on flattened paper muffin cups. Refrigerate for several hours (at least 2). Burgers can be refrigerated for 2 to 3 days.

To serve, sauté burgers in a lightly oiled frying pan until brown and medium rare. Burgers can also be broiled.

Lamb Burgers are delicious served on pita bread and topped with Tzatzíki Sauce. (See Index.)

Makes 2¼ pounds.

LIVERWURST

If you find yourself buying liverwurst often, try making your own for a change. This recipe will provide you with a savory, but much less expensive variety.

1 pound pork liver
8 ounces pork shoulder
6 ounces pork fat
1 bottle stout (dark beer)
½ cup chopped onion
1 tablespoon vegetable oil
1 tablespoon coarse salt

1 teaspoon sugar
1 teaspoon dry mustard
1 teaspoon freshly ground
   black pepper
1 teaspoon thyme
¼ teaspoon ground ginger
¼ teaspoon marjoram

Cover pork liver, pork shoulder, and fat with stout in a large saucepan or Dutch oven.

Heat mixture to simmering; simmer about 50 minutes. Remove from heat; place meats and stock in a large bowl. Cool. Refrigerate covered overnight.

Sauté onions in oil, until soft but not brown; cool. Strain meats, reserving stock. Grind meats using smallest hole plate available on grinder. Regrind. (This step is best done in a food processor, processing meat through the feed tube with the steel knife rotating. Process until mixture forms a paste.)

Mix salt, sugar, and spices in a small bowl. Add to meat mixture with ⅓ cup of the reserved stock. Beat mixture well with wooden spoon or continue with one or two spurts in the food processor.

Place a 12-inch piece of plastic wrap on a flat surface. Place mixture on wrap; form into a roll 12 inches long, 3 inches in diameter. Wrap roll and twist ends tightly. Refrigerate liverwurst until very cold. Slice and serve cold. Liverwurst can be refrigerated for about 1 week.

Makes 2 pounds.

LIVER TERRINE—OLD VIENNA STYLE

This recipe was supplied by Anton Hink of Vienna, of the firm of Hink Vienna, makers of fine pâtés, terrines, and quality meat items found in the fine shops of Europe like Fauchon in Paris and Käfer-Schänke of Munich. The elegant terrine is for people who enjoy specialty foods.

1 pound pork liver
½ pound calves' liver
1½ pounds lean pork
3 cloves garlic, sliced
½ cup chopped shallots or
   onions
3 bay leaves
3 large sprigs parsley
1 tablespoon coarse salt
2 teaspoons freshly ground
   black pepper

2 teaspoons marjoram
About 1 cup dry white
   wine
3 large eggs
⅓ cup brandy
½ cup finely chopped fresh
   parsley
1 teaspoon marjoram
1 teaspoon coarse salt
1 pound pork belly or
   blanched bacon

Dice the pork and calves' livers, and pork. Mix diced meats, garlic, shallots, bay leaves, parsley sprigs, 1 tablespoon salt, the pepper, and 2 teaspoons marjoram in a large bowl. Cover with wine; refrigerate mixture and allow to marinate overnight.

Drain meat mixture well; discard the wine, bay leaves, and parsley sprigs. Dry the meat mixture in paper toweling. Grind mixture twice, first using the large hole plate on grinder and then using the small hole plate. If the texture is not fine, grind once more. Add the eggs, brandy, chopped parsley, 1 teaspoon marjoram, and 1 teaspoon salt. Beat well. Line an earthenware mold with half the slices of pork belly or blanched bacon. (To blanch bacon, place in boiling water two minutes.) Place meat mixture in the mold, packing it well and up to the top of the mold. Cover with remaining pork belly or blanched bacon. Cover mold with aluminum foil.

Place the mold in a larger pan of very hot water so the water level reaches three-fourths of the way up the sides of the mold. Bake mold in pan at 300° for about 2½ hours. If a cooking thermometer is available, it should register 170° when inserted in the center of the mold.

Remove pan from oven; remove mold from water bath. Immediately place a baking sheet topped with a heavy weight on mold to compress the terrine. Cool. When the terrine is cold, refrigerate with the weight overnight. Let terrine ripen at least 24 hours in refrigerator before serving.

To serve, remove the fat from the terrine; spread on tasty breads. The remainder can be refrigerated tightly wrapped until later serving but no longer than one week. The terrine is delicious as an appetizer or luncheon item served with spicy black olives.

Makes 2½ pounds.

LUGANEGA SAUSAGE

Pat Bruno, author, cook, and instructor, provided this recipe. It makes a mild-seasoned, delicate Italian sausage, perfect for breakfast.

2 pounds pork shoulder	¼ teaspoon ground coriander
½ pound veal shoulder or breast	¼ teaspoon ground oregano
2 ice cubes	2 tablespoons freshly grated Parmesan cheese
1 tablespoon coarse salt	
½ teaspoon freshly ground black pepper	About 50 inches natural pork casings

Grind pork and veal together using the large hole plate on grinder. Add ice cubes during grinding to keep meats cold and clear grinder. Mix salt, spices, and cheese in a small bowl. Add to ground meats; mix well. Refrigerate 1 to 2 hours.

Prepare casings according to instructions. (See Index.)

Sauté a small amount of sausage in a lightly oiled frying pan until thoroughly cooked. Taste and adjust seasonings, if desired.

Stuff sausage into casings according to manufacturer's instructions that accompany grinder or use hand stuffing funnel. Do not overstuff.

Refrigerate sausage uncovered several hours, turning sausage once during that period.

To serve, simmer sausage in water to cover for about 10 minutes. Drain and dry. Sauté sausage in lightly oiled frying pan until brown and thoroughly cooked. Sausage can be refrigerated 1 or 2 days, or frozen for longer periods.

Makes 2½ pounds.

MAHNEEK

Mahneek is an interesting lamb sausage which you will serve often after your first experience. This sausage has long been enjoyed in the Middle East and should certainly tantalize American tastebuds.

2 pounds lamb shoulder or
   breast, including about
   ½ pound fat
2 to 3 ice cubes
1 tablespoon coarse salt
1 teaspoon sugar
1 teaspoon coarsely ground
   black pepper
1 teaspoon rosemary
½ teaspoon Greek oregano

½ teaspoon ground cloves
¼ teaspoon ground allspice
⅓ cup dry red wine
   (Zinfandel, Burgundy)
4 cloves garlic, finely
   minced or pressed
50 inches natural pork
   casings
Additional wine to cover
   sausage (optional)

Grind lamb and fat twice using the small hole plate on grinder. Add ice cubes during grinding to keep meat cold and clear grinder. Refrigerate ground lamb. Mix salt, sugar, and spices in a small bowl. Add to ground lamb. Add wine and garlic; mix thoroughly.

Prepare casings according to instructions. (See Index.)

Sauté a small amount of sausage in a lightly oiled frying pan. Taste and adjust seasonings, if desired.

Stuff sausage into casings according to manufacturer's instructions that accompany grinder or use hand stuffing funnel. Let sausage ripen in refrigerator several hours, turning once during that period. (It is preferable after stuffing casings to place sausage in a large bowl and cover with wine. Let soak for several hours or longer depending on taste desired. Drain; discard wine and then let ripen as instructed.)

To serve, sauté sausage in a lightly oiled frying pan until brown. (It is not necessary to cook thoroughly as in pork sausage. Lamb is best eaten underdone.)

Makes 2 pounds.

MIDWESTERN SAUSAGE

This sausage will please the palates of people of any region, with its unusual blend of spices and herbs.

1½ pounds pork shoulder
½ pound pork fat
2 ice cubes
2 teaspoons coarse salt
1 teaspoon dehydrated
  minced onions
2 tablespoons water
1 teaspoon sugar
2 teaspoons sage

1 teaspoon hot paprika
1 teaspoon freshly ground
  coarse black pepper
1 teaspoon marjoram
1 teaspoon summer savory
½ teaspoon thyme
50 inches natural pork
  casings

Grind pork and pork fat together using the large hole plate on grinder. Add ice cubes during grinding to keep meat cold and clear grinder. Regrind using the small hole plate on grinder. Add salt; mix thoroughly.

Reconstitute onions in water in a small bowl. Mix sugar and spices in a second small bowl. Add onions and spice mixture to pork mixture; mix thoroughly. Refrigerate covered 1 or 2 hours.

Prepare casings according to instructions. (See Index.) Sauté a small amount of sausage in a lightly oiled frying pan until thoroughly cooked. Taste and adjust seasonings, if desired.

Stuff sausage into casings according to manufacturer's instructions that acompany grinder or use hand stuffing funnel. Do not overstuff. Refrigerate sausage uncovered, several hours, turning once during that period.

To serve, sauté sausage in a lightly oiled frying pan until thoroughly cooked. Serve for breakfast, lunch, or dinner, or in any recipe calling for a mild-flavored sausage.

Makes 2 pounds.

MILD ITALIAN SAUSAGE

You will use this versatile sausage often in spaghetti sauce, pizza topping, or casserole dishes such as lasagna.

1½ pounds pork shoulder
½ pound pork fat
2 ice cubes
2 teaspoons salt
1 teaspoon fennel seed, crushed
½ teaspoon ground red pepper

½ teaspoon sweet paprika
½ teaspoon freshly ground black pepper
½ teaspoon sugar
⅛ teaspoon chili powder

Grind pork and pork fat using the large hole plate on grinder. Add ice cubes during grinding to keep meat cold and clear grinder. Add salt; mix well.

Mix remaining ingredients in a small bowl. Add to ground pork; mix again. Refrigerate mixture covered at least 2 hours.

Sauté a small amount of sausage in a lightly oiled frying pan until thoroughly cooked. Taste and adjust seasonings, if desired.

Sausage can be refrigerated for 1 or 2 days or frozen for longer periods. Casings may be filled with this sausage, if desired. Follow instructions in Hot Italian Sausage recipe. (See Index.)

Makes 2 pounds.

MILD ITALIAN SAUSAGE—NO FENNEL

This tasty sausage is for those who prefer sausage without the flavor of fennel.

1½ pounds pork shoulder
½ pound pork fat
2 ice cubes
2 teaspoons coarse salt
½ teaspoon sugar
½ teaspoon ground red
    pepper

½ teaspoon coarsely ground
    black pepper
¼ teaspoon chili powder
¼ teaspoon hot paprika
¼ teaspoon celery seed
50 inches natural pork
    casings

Grind pork and pork fat, using the large hole plate on grinder. Add ice cubes during grinding to keep meat cold and clear grinder. Add salt to ground pork; mix thoroughly. Mix sugar and spices in a small bowl. Add spice mixture to meat mixture; mix thoroughly. If mixture seems dry, add a small amount of water and mix again. Refrigerate covered for 2 hours.

Prepare casings according to instructions. (See Index.)

Sauté a small amount of sausage in a lightly oiled frying pan until thoroughly cooked. Taste and adjust seasonings, if desired.

Stuff sausage into casings using a hand stuffing funnel. This will retain coarse texture of ground pork.

To form links, place length of sausage on a flat surface; twist in center. Then begin twisting together 2-inch lengths, one from each side of the center twist. Continue until all links are twisted. Refrigerate sausage uncovered for several hours, turning once during that period.

Use sausage in any recipe calling for Italian sausage.

Makes 2 pounds.

MILWAUKEE SAUSAGE

Beer and sausage are favorite "go-togethers" in Milwaukee. In this recipe they are combined to make a delicious sausage.

2 pounds pork loin end or
    Boston butt
½ pound pork fat
12 ounces beer
2½ teaspoons salt
1 teaspoon sugar
1 tablespoon coarsely
    ground black pepper

4 teaspoons dill seed
2 teaspoons hot paprika
1½ teaspoons dry mustard
1 teaspoon summer savory
About 50 inches natural
    pork casings

Cut pork and fat into small pieces. Place in a large bowl; cover with beer. Let pork marinate covered in the refrigerator at least 24 hours. Drain pork and discard beer. Dry pork. Grind using coarse plate.

Mix salt, sugar, spices, and herbs in a small bowl. Add to pork; mix thoroughly. Refrigerate.

Prepare casings according to instructions. (See Index.) Stuff sausage into casings according to manufacturer's instructions that accompany grinder or use hand stuffing funnel. Refrigerate sausage uncovered several hours (at least 2), then turn. Refrigerate overnight.

To serve, sauté sausage in a lightly oiled frying pan until brown and thoroughly cooked. Serve sausage with sauerkraut and German potato salad.

Makes 2½ pounds.

MÜNCHEN SAUSAGE

This delicate sausage is a favorite of Munich. Our version is made with pork instead of veal, lightly seasoned, and flavored with fresh lemon. We consider this sausage too fragile for casings.

2 pounds pork loin meat
½ pound pork fat
1 tablespoon coarse salt
Rind of 2 lemons
2 tablespoons water

½ cup finely chopped fresh parsley
2 teaspoons coarsely ground black pepper

Cut the pork and fat into pieces small enough to place in grinder hopper. Grind using the large hole plate on grinder. Add salt; mix thoroughly. Refrigerate covered for several hours.

Grate lemon rind. Add water to rind. Add rind, parsley, and pepper to pork mixture. Mix thoroughly. Regrind mixture using the small hole plate on grinder. Refrigerate sausage covered for several hours (at least 2).

Place stuffer on grinder according to manufacturer's instructions. Place sausage in hopper and let run through stuffer without casings. Place 6-inch pieces on plate or Styrofoam trays which have been saved from meat purchases and washed. Cover links; refrigerate until ready to use. Sausage can be refrigerated for 2 days or frozen 3 to 4 weeks.

To serve, sauté sausage in a lightly oiled frying pan until brown but not dry. This sausage is delicious served with softly cooked scrambled eggs or fruit pancakes.

Makes 2½ pounds.

PARISIENNE SAUSAGE

A sausage made with a blend of beef, pork, and aromatic spices, will provide a mild yet flavorful breakfast or luncheon item.

1¼ pounds pork loin ends
¾ pound beef chuck
½ pound pork fat
2 ice cubes
2½ teaspoons salt
½ teaspoon sugar
1 tablespoon freshly ground
    black pepper
1 teaspoon ground nutmeg
1 teaspoon summer savory
½ teaspoon ground cloves

½ teaspoon mace
½ teaspoon ground thyme
½ teaspoon ground ginger
½ teaspoon ground
    cinnamon
½ teaspoon ground bay leaf
    or 1 bay leaf, very
    finely crumbled
50 inches natural pork
    casings

Grind pork and beef together using the large hole plate on grinder. Grind fat using the small hole plate on grinder. Add ice cubes during grinding to keep meats cold, clear grinder, and provide moisture for seasonings.

Mix salt, sugar, spices, and herbs in small bowl. Add to ground meats; mix well. Refrigerate for several hours.

Sauté a small amount of sausage in a lightly oiled frying pan until thoroughly cooked. Taste and adjust seasonings, if desired.

Prepare casings according to instructions. (See Index.) Stuff sausage into casings using manufacturer's instructions that accompany grinder or use hand stuffing funnel.

Sausage can be refrigerated for 2 to 3 days or frozen for longer periods. To serve, sauté sausage in a lightly oiled frying pan until brown and thoroughly cooked.

Makes 2½ pounds.

PASTITSIO SAUSAGE

If you have enjoyed the famous Greek dish Pastitsio, this sausage will provide you with all the same flavors. Serve it with mostaccioli in a cheese sauce and you will have a close version of the original dish.

1½ pounds lamb shoulder, including some fat
½ pound beef chuck, including some fat
2 teaspoons coarse salt
1 tablespoon tomato sauce or 2 teaspoons tomato paste
½ cup dry white wine
1 teaspoon ground cinnamon
¼ teaspoon ground nutmeg
1 tablespoon dehydrated minced onions
2 tablespoons cold water
1 clove garlic, finely minced or pressed
2 tablespoons Romano, Parmesan, or Kefaltori cheese (imported preferred)
50 inches natural pork casings

Grind lamb and beef together using large hole plate on grinder. Add salt, tomato sauce, and wine; mix thoroughly. Add cinnamon and nutmeg. Reconstitute onions in cold water in a small bowl. Add garlic to onions; mix well. Add to meat mixture. Add cheese; mix all ingredients thoroughly. Refrigerate.

Prepare casings according to instructions. (See Index.)

Sauté a small amount of sausage in a lightly oiled frying pan. Taste and adjust seasonings, if desired.

Stuff sausage into casings according to manufacturer's instructions that accompany grinder or use hand stuffing funnel.

Sausage can be refrigerated 2 to 3 days or frozen for longer periods. You may use it as a loose sausage if it will be used to make Pastitsio (see Pastitsio in Index).

Makes 2 pounds.

PÂTÉ DE CAMPAGNE

This wonderful pâté recipe was supplied by Mrs. Denise Guback who teaches French courses at the University of Illinois in Champaign. Bertie's daughter, Martha, was her student. In Madame Guback's household, there is always a pâté de campagne in the refrigerator. Try it for your family and for parties, too.

½ pound veal meat (breast of veal preferred)
½ pound pork shoulder or pork loin end
½ pound smoked or boiled ham
2 chicken livers
2 cloves garlic, finely minced or pressed
¼ cup evaporated milk
2 eggs
¼ cup cognac or brandy
2 teaspoons coarse salt

1 teaspoon freshly ground black pepper
¼ cup flour (instant type preferred)
¼ teaspoon ground allspice
¼ cup chopped fresh parsley
2 tablespoons chopped fresh herbs, such as basil, oregano, thyme, marjoram, if available (do not use dry)
5 bay leaves

Grind veal, pork, ham, and livers together using the large hole plate on grinder. Regrind using the small hole plate on grinder. (This could best be done in a food processor, processing meats through feed tube with steel knife rotating.) Add remaining ingredients, except bay leaves, to ground meats; beat until mixture forms a mass.

Generously butter a loaf pan, 8½ × 5 × 3 inches. Spoon meat mixture into pan, pushing down on mixture with a spatula. Place bay leaves on pâté. Cover with aluminum foil. Preheat oven to 325°. Place filled loaf pan in a larger pan of hot water, so water level reaches about two-thirds of the way up the sides of the loaf pan.

Bake pâté for about 1½ hours; uncover and bake 15 to 20 minutes longer to brown. When done, metal skewer inserted in pâté should come out clean. If a cooking thermometer is available, it should register 160° when inserted in the center of the pâté. Remove pâté from oven and from water bath. Remove bay leaves; cover pâté again with aluminum foil. Place a heavy weight on the pâté to compress it to facilitate slicing later. Cool pâté; then refrigerate at least 12 hours before slicing. Slice pâté and serve cold.

Makes 2 pounds.

QUICK CHILI SAUSAGE

When people think of chili, beef comes to mind as one of the major ingredients. For a pleasant change, try this recipe made with pork instead.

1 pound ground pork
**   mixed with pork fat**
1 package chili mix
¼ cup water

Mix pork, chili mix, and water in a large bowl. Refrigerate at least one hour. Pork mixture can be made into a sausage roll as follows: Place an 18-inch piece of plastic wrap on a flat surface. Place refrigerated pork mixture on wrap; shape into a roll 12 inches long and 3 inches in diameter. Refrigerate roll until very cold. Slice sausage; sauté in a lightly oiled frying pan until thoroughly cooked. This may also be sautéed as a loose sausage, and add beans for a chili meal.

Sausage can be refrigerated, cooked or uncooked, for several days or frozen for longer periods.

Makes 1¼ pounds.

QUICK ONION SAUSAGE PATTIES

These patties are a change of pace from hamburger. Served with or without rolls, they are equally delicious.

½ cup dehydrated minced
    onions
¼ cup cold water
2 pounds ground pork, with
    some fat ground in the
    pork

1 tablespoon poultry
    seasoning
2 teaspoons salt
1 teaspoon sugar
½ teaspoon hot paprika

Reconstitute onions in water. Combine onions and remaining ingredients in a large bowl until thoroughly mixed.

Place two 12-inch pieces of plastic wrap on a flat surface. Divide meat mixture in half; place each half on piece of plastic wrap. Form each half into a roll about 3 inches in diameter. Wrap sausage and twist ends tightly. Roll on table to compact the sausage. Refrigerate at least 12 hours before slicing.

Slice sausage. Sauté sausage in a lightly oiled frying pan, or broil, until brown and thoroughly cooked.

Serve on a round roll or as the meat item for any meal.

Note: Be sure the poultry seasoning contains sage, thyme, marjoram, black pepper, and nutmeg.

Makes 2 pounds.

ROUNDETTES

You will find this recipe a welcome alternative to hamburgers. Roundettes are savory, served on a roll, and won't even need condiments.

1½ pounds pork shoulder
1 pound beef chuck
4 ounces pork fat or a
   combination of beef and
   pork fat
2 teaspoons coarse salt
2 tablespoons dehydrated
   minced onions
¼ cup water
½ teaspoon sugar

1 teaspoon ground black
   pepper
⅛ teaspoon ground nutmeg
½ teaspoon summer savory
½ teaspoon sage
½ teaspoon celery seed
¼ teaspoon ground red
   pepper
¼ teaspoon hot paprika

Grind pork, beef, and fat together using the large hole plate on grinder. Add salt; mix thoroughly. Cover mixture and refrigerate. Refrigerate assembled grinder for second grinding.

Reconstitute onions in water in a small bowl. Mix sugar and spices in a second small bowl.

Regrind meat mixture using the small hole plate on grinder. Add onions and spice mixture to meat mixture; mix thoroughly.

Sauté a small amount of sausage in a lightly oiled frying pan until thoroughly cooked. Taste and adjust seasonings, if desired. Refrigerate mixture for several hours or until thoroughly chilled.

Place two 18-inch sheets of wax paper on a flat surface. Spread sausage on 1 sheet; cover with second sheet. Roll out sausage with rolling pin to about 1-inch thickness. With a 3-inch cutter, cut sausage into circles until all meat is shaped (about 14 to 16 Roundettes). Place each Roundette on a flattened paper muffin cup; refrigerate until serving time. Roundettes can be frozen for longer periods.

To serve, prepare and use as hamburgers.

Note: A tuna fish can or similar size can makes an excellent cutter. With a can opener cutting with a smooth surface edge, remove both the top and bottom of the can. Wash can thoroughly, if necessary with baking soda, and use as a cutter. For larger size Roundettes, use a large size tuna can.

Makes 2¾ pounds.

SAVORY BRATWURST

This is a lightly seasoned bratwurst, made with the best cut of pork together with veal—a combination you will find delectable.

1¼ pounds center pork loin
½ pound veal breast,
    trimmed, fat reserved
¼ pound pork and veal fat
3 ice cubes
2 teaspoons coarse salt
1 teaspoon sugar

2 teaspoons freshly ground
    white pepper
½ teaspoon mace
½ teaspoon ground nutmeg
½ teaspoon celery seed
½ teaspoon dry mustard
About 50 inches natural
    pork casings

Grind meats and fats together using the large hole plate on grinder. Add ice cubes during grinding to keep meats cold and clear grinder. Add salt; mix thoroughly. Refrigerate covered at least 1 hour. Refrigerate assembled grinder for second grinding.

Mix sugar and spices in a small bowl. Add to ground meats; mix thoroughly. Sauté a small amount of sausage in a lightly oiled frying pan until thoroughly cooked. Taste and adjust seasonings, if desired. Refrigerate 2 to 3 hours. Regrind meat mixture using the small hole plate on grinder.

Prepare casings according to instructions. (See Index.) Stuff sausage into casings according to manufacturer's instructions that accompany grinder or use hand stuffing funnel.

To serve, sauté sausage slowly in a lightly oiled frying pan until brown and thoroughly cooked.

Makes 2 pounds.

SCANDINAVIAN POTATO SAUSAGE

This sausage tastes much like freshly made hash. It is good at dinner or luncheon, served with sautéed apples.

4 medium potatoes, pared,
    cut up
1½ pounds beef pork
1 pound pork shoulder or
    ends of pork loin
2 medium onions
2 tablespoons coarse salt

1 teaspoon ground allspice
1 teaspoon freshly ground
    black pepper
1 teaspoon sugar
60 inches pork casings
2 teaspoons salt

Blanch potatoes in boiling water for about 5 minutes. Drain and cool.

Grind meats, potatoes, and onions using the large hole plate on grinder. Add 2 tablespoons salt; mix thoroughly. Refrigerate.

Prepare casings according to instructions. (See Index.) Add allspice, pepper, and sugar to meat mixture; mix thoroughly.

Sauté a small amount of sausage in a lightly oiled frying pan until thoroughly cooked. Taste and adjust seasonings, if desired.

Stuff sausage into casings according to manufacturer's instructions that accompany grinder or use hand stuffing funnel. Do not overstuff or casings will burst during cooking. There must be room for potatoes to expand during cooking period.

To form links, place length of sausage on a flat surface. Twist in center. Then begin twisting together 2-inch lengths, one from each side of the center twist. Continue until all links are twisted. In a large bowl, place sausage; water to cover. Add 2 teaspoons of salt. Cover bowl until serving time. (This will prevent potatoes from darkening.)

Sausage can be refrigerated for several days. Do not freeze or potatoes will become very soft and unpalatable.

To serve, simmer sausage in water to cover in a deep frying pan for 20 to 30 minutes. Drain. Sausage can be sautéed after draining, if desired.

Makes 3 pounds.

SCRAPPLE

If you have been saving your pork bones, now is the time to use them. Scrapple is a longtime breakfast favorite in many homes, served with pure maple syrup or honey.

4 cups Pork Stock (recipe
   follows)
1 cup yellow cornmeal
1 cup cold water
1 teaspoon salt

1 tablespoon grated onion
½ teaspoon sage
½ teaspoon sweet paprika
Flour (instant type
   preferred)

Make Pork Stock.

Mix cornmeal, cold water, and salt. Heat pork stock in a heavy-duty pan to boiling. Pour cornmeal mixture into boiling stock, stirring with a wire whisk until it returns to a boil. Reduce heat; simmer, stirring occasionally (be very careful that boiling mixture does not bubble up and burn you) for about 10 minutes. Remove from heat.

Finely mince or coarsely grind the reserved meat from stock. Add meat, grated onion, sage, and paprika to cooked cornmeal mixture.

Line a loaf pan, 8½ × 5 × 3 inches, with plastic wrap; coat with a small amount of vegetable oil. Pour cornmeal mixture into pan; cover with plastic wrap. Cool; refrigerate for several hours.

To serve; slice Scrapple and coat with flour. Sauté in equal amounts of oil and butter in a frying pan until brown. Serve hot with syrup or honey for breakfast or lunch.

Makes 2 pounds.

PORK STOCK

This stock is also delicious used for bean soup. So double the recipe to have enough on hand.

Pork bones, with meat on
   the bones
2 quarts water

1 onion, stuck with 2 or 3
   whole cloves
1 bay leaf

Heat pork bones and water to boiling in a large saucepan or

Dutch oven; reduce heat. Remove raft (foam) from stock. Add onion and bay leaf (do not add salt). Simmer for about 1 hour or until meat loosens from bones. Remove bones from stock; separate meat from bones and reserve. Strain stock. Refrigerate to remove excessive fat. Discard fat. Use stock immediately or freeze for later use.

SCRAPPLE—ALTERNATE METHOD

Try this recipe for hurry-up times. It makes a very tasty and nutritious scrapple.

½ pound Favorite Breakfast
　Sausage (see Index)
1 cup yellow cornmeal
4 cups cold water
1 teaspoon salt

½ cup water
1 tablespoon finely minced
　onion
Flour (instant type
　preferred)

Make Favorite Breakfast Sausage, except do not sauté.

Mix cornmeal, 1 cup of the cold water, and the salt. Heat remaining 3 cups cold water in a heavy-duty pan to boiling. Pour cornmeal mixture into boiling water, stirring with a wire whisk until it returns to a boil. Reduce heat; simmer, stirring occasionally (be very careful that boiling mixture does not bubble up and burn you), for about 10 minutes.

While cornmeal is cooking, cook sausage with ½ cup water in a frying pan, breaking up sausage meat while cooking. Reduce heat; simmer until sausage is cooked. Add sausage with water in which it was cooked and onion to cooked cornmeal. Mix thoroughly.

Line a loaf pan, 8½ × 5 × 3 inches, with plastic wrap; coat with a small amount of vegetable oil. Pour cornmeal-sausage mixture into pan; cover with plastic wrap. Cool; refrigerate for several hours.

To serve, slice scrapple and coat with flour. Sauté in equal amounts of oil and butter in a frying pan until brown. Serve hot with syrup or honey for breakfast or lunch.

Makes 2 pounds.

SEED SAUSAGE

This is an unusual recipe to add to your repertoire. Sample it once and you will make it often. It's delicious for any meal but try it for dinner with creamy mashed potatoes.

2 pounds pork loin end or
    pork shoulder
½ pound pork fat
4 ice cubes
2½ teaspoons coarse salt
1 teaspoon celery seed
1 teaspoon mustard seed
1 teaspoon sesame seed
1 tablespoon cold water

1 teaspoon sugar
1 teaspoon coarsely ground
    black pepper
1 teaspoon hot paprika
1 teaspoon ground coriander
½ teaspoon summer savory
    (fresh, if available)
50 inches natural pork
    casings

Grind pork and pork fat together using the large hole plate on grinder. Add ice cubes during grinding to keep meat cold and clear grinder. Add salt; mix thoroughly.

Mix celery, mustard, and sesame seeds in a small bowl. Add cold water to soften. Add sugar and spices. Let stand 10 minutes; add to pork mixture. Cover; refrigerate for several hours.

Prepare casings according to instructions. (See Index.)

Sauté a small amount of sausage in a lightly oiled frying pan until thoroughly cooked. Taste and adjust seasonings, if desired. Stuff sausage into casings according to manufacturer's instructions that accompany grinder or use hand stuffing funnel. Refrigerate sausage uncovered for several hours, turning once during that period. Sausage can be refrigerated 2 to 3 days or frozen for longer periods.

To serve, sauté sausage slowly in a lightly oiled frying pan until brown and thoroughly cooked.

Makes 2½ pounds.

SIMPLE SAUSAGE

A good friend, Betty Marshall, suggested this quick and easy recipe for times when seasonings are hard to obtain. When she and her husband lived in Iran, they were not able to purchase the usual spices for sausage. She tried and liked poultry seasoning as a substitute.

2 pounds pork shoulder,
   ground
¼ cup cold water
2 teaspoons salt

1 teaspoon sugar
2 teaspoons poultry
   seasoning

Mix ground pork, cold water, salt, sugar, and seasoning in a large bowl; mix thoroughly.

Place two 12-inch pieces of plastic wrap on a flat surface. Divide meat mixture in half. Place each half on plastic wrap, shaping into a roll of desired thickness. Wrap each roll and twist ends tightly. Roll sausage several times to compact meat. Refrigerate sausage at least 12 hours before slicing for cooking. Sausage can be refrigerated 2 to 3 days or frozen for longer periods.

To serve, slice sausage. Sauté sausage in a lightly oiled frying pan until brown and thoroughly cooked.

Note: Read the label when purchasing poultry seasoning to be sure it contains sage, thyme, marjoram, rosemary, black pepper, and nutmeg, or at least most of these spices.

Makes 2 pounds.

SPAGHETTI SAUSAGE

For those who like meatballs or sausage with their spaghetti, this is the recipe for you—a meatball sausage. Try it in a sandwich on hard-crusted Italian bread, too.

2 teaspoons salt (1 teaspoon salt if cheese is salty)
½ teaspoon freshly ground black pepper
½ teaspoon Italian herb (available in the spice rack in supermarkets)
1½ pounds ground beef
½ pound ground pork shoulder
2 large eggs, lightly beaten
⅓ cup freshly grated Parmesan or Romano cheese

2 slices firm-textured fresh bread (Italian or French) shredded or crumbled (food processor is marvelous for this)
2 to 3 cloves garlic, finely minced or pressed
¼ cup finely chopped fresh parsley
About 60 inches natural pork casings

Blend salt, pepper, and Italian seasoning in a small bowl. Combine beef and pork in a large bowl. Add eggs, cheese, herb mixture, and bread; blend thoroughly. If mixture seems dry, add two tablespoons water and mix again. Refrigerate sausage for about 1 hour.

Sauté a small amount of sausage in a lightly oiled frying pan until thoroughly cooked. Taste and adjust seasonings, if desired.

Prepare casings according to instructions. (See Index.) Stuff sausage into casings according to manufacturer's instructions that accompany grinder or use hand stuffing funnel. Refrigerate until ready to use but no longer than 2 or 3 days.

To serve, see Index for Sausage Spaghetti Sauce recipe.

Note: Fresh parsley will keep for about 2 weeks if it is refrigerated in a glass jar. Do not wash parsley until ready to use or it will decay.

Makes 2 pounds.

SÜLTZ

The recipe for this delicious cold meat was supplied by a good friend Irene Chmura. It has been enjoyed in her family for two generations and this version is modernized with today's ingredients. Sültz is a great buffet party item.

2 pounds veal shoulder or
    veal breast
2 pounds fresh pork hocks
1 pig's foot, split
6 cups cold water, or
    enough to cover the
    meats
½ cup distilled white
    vinegar
5 sprigs fresh parsley
3 large bay leaves
1 teaspoon whole allspice
1 teaspoon whole peppercorns

½ cup coarsely chopped
    celery, including leaves
1 onion, cut into quarters,
    stuck with 2 whole
    cloves
1½ to 2 teaspoons coarse
    salt
2 to 3 teaspoons gelatin
¼ cup cold stock
Pimiento-stuffed olives
    (optional)
Vegetable oil

Combine meats and cold water in a stock pot or Dutch oven. Heat to boiling. Skim to remove the raft (foam); reduce heat. Add ¼ cup of the vinegar, parsley, bay leaves, allspice, peppercorns, celery, and onion. Heat mixture to boiling; reduce heat to simmering. Cover and simmer until all meats are tender. (Pierce with the point of a sharp knife to test for doneness.)

Remove meats from the stock. Strain stock. Discard spices and vegetables. Return stock to heat; cook until stock is reduced to about 3 cups. Add salt.

Finely dice meats. Discard any fat but include all pork rind; reserve. Soften gelatin in ¼ cup cold stock. Add softened gelatin and remaining ¼ cup vinegar to the reduced stock. Taste and adjust for salt and tartness. Add reserved meats to stock. Pour stock and meats into a lightly oiled loaf pan, 8½ × 4 × 3 inches. Refrigerate until entire contents have set completely.

To serve, slice thinly. Use as an appetizer or as cold meat for luncheon, served wtih a tasty potato salad. For more color and flavor, add ½ cup chopped pimiento-stuffed olives. Sültz can be refrigerated about 1 week; do not freeze.

Makes 3 pounds.

SUNDAY BREAKFAST SAUSAGE

This recipe combines breakfast favorites ham and bacon in a tasty, mildly seasoned sausage.

1½ pounds pork shoulder or pork loin ends
½ pound ham
½ pound bacon
3 to 4 ice cubes
1 teaspoon salt
1 tablespoon dehydrated minced onions
3 tablespoons water
1 teaspoon sugar

1 teaspoon dry mustard
1 teaspoon freshly ground black pepper
½ teaspoon sage
½ teaspoon summer savory
½ teaspoon ground red pepper
½ teaspoon thyme
¼ teaspoon ground ginger
50 inches natural pork casings

Grind pork, ham, and bacon together using the large hole plate on grinder. Regrind using 1 or 2 ice cubes. Add salt; mix thoroughly. Refrigerate. Reconstitute onions in water.

Blend sugar and spices in a small bowl. Add onions and spice combination to meat mixture. Mix thoroughly; refrigerate.

Sauté a small amount of sausage in a lightly oiled frying pan until thoroughly cooked. Taste and adjust seasonings, if desired.

Prepare casings according to instructions. (See Index.)

Stuff sausage into casings according to manufacturer's instructions that accompany grinder or use hand stuffing funnel. Do not overstuff or it will not be possible to form into links. Use ice cubes to clear grinder and funnel.

To form links, place length of sausage on a flat surface. Twist in center. Then begin twisting together 2-inch lengths, one from each side of the center twist. Continue until all links are twisted. Refrigerate uncovered for at least several hours, or overnight, turning once during that period.

To serve, simmer sausage in water to cover in frying pan for 5 minutes. Do not boil or casings will burst. Turn sausage during simmering period if necessary. Drain. Dry pan with paper towel. Sauté sausage slowly in lightly oiled frying pan until thoroughly cooked. Ham will remain pink even when sausage is cooked. Sausage can be refrigerated for 2 to 3 days.

Note: Some supermarkets sell bacon ends and ham ends at a reduced price.

Makes 2½ pounds.

TACO SAUSAGE

You will enjoy the uniqueness of this sausage and the method of serving it. The spices used will appeal to most palates. The sausage is convenient to freeze and have available for quick meals and hungry teenagers.

1 pound pork
½ pound beef chuck
½ pound pork fat
2 ice cubes, crushed if necessary
2 teaspoons coarse salt
1 tablespoon dehydrated minced onions
3 tablespoons water
2 cloves fresh garlic, finely minced or pressed

2 teaspoons chili powder
1 teaspoon hot paprika
1 teaspoon ground red pepper
1 teaspoon crushed red pepper
½ teaspoon oregano (Greek variety preferred)
½ teaspoon cumin
1 teaspoon sugar
About 50 inches natural pork casings

Grind the meats and fat together using the large hole plate on grinder. Add 1 ice cube to grinder when half the meat is ground and again when grinding is completed. Add salt; mix well. Refrigerate 2 to 3 hours.

Reconstitute onions in water in a small bowl. Add garlic to onions; stir. Mix spices and sugar in a small bowl.

Prepare casings according to instructions. (See Index.) Add onion mixture and spice mixture to ground meats; mix thoroughly. Refrigerate for about 1 hour.

Sauté a small amount of sausage in a lightly oiled frying pan until thoroughly cooked. Taste and adjust seasonings, if desired.

Stuff sausage into casings according to manufacturer's instructions that accompany grinder or use hand stuffing funnel. Refrigerate until ready to use but no longer than 2 days. Sausage can be frozen for longer periods.

To serve, sauté sausage slowly in a lightly oiled frying pan until brown and thoroughly cooked. For additional serving suggestion see Index for recipe for Tacos.

Makes 2½ pounds.

TRI-MEAT SAUSAGE

The variety of meats gives this lightly seasoned sausage a unique taste.

1 pound pork shoulder
½ pound veal breast
½ pound beef chuck
¼ pound pork, beef, or veal
    fat, or a combination
2 ice cubes
2 teaspoons coarse salt
1 teaspoon coarsely ground
    black pepper

1 teaspoon summer savory
1 teaspoon marjoram
½ teaspoon hot paprika
½ teaspoon ground nutmeg
1 teaspoon sugar
About 50 inches natural
    pork casings

Grind all meats using the large hole plate on grinder. Regrind using the small hole plate on grinder. Add ice cubes during grinding to keep meats cold, add moisture to the seasonings, and clear grinder. Add salt; mix well. Refrigerate.

Prepare casings according to instructions. (See Index.)

Mix all spices and sugar in a small bowl. Add to ground meats; mix thoroughly. Refrigerate meat mixture; refrigerate grinder head.

Sauté a small amount of sausage in a lightly oiled frying pan until thoroughly cooked. Taste and adjust seasonings, if desired.

Stuff sausage into casings according to manufacturer's instructions that accompany grinder or use hand stuffer. Refrigerate sausage uncovered for several hours, turning once during that period.

Sausage can also be put in a roll, "country style." Place two 12-inch pieces of plastic wrap on a flat surface. Place half the sausage on each piece of wrap. Form a long roll about 8 inches long or the diameter of the slice you desire. Wrap sausage and twist ends tightly.

Refrigerate sausage overnight before using. Sausage can be refrigerated for 3 days or frozen for 3 weeks.

Makes 2½ pounds.

VENISON AND BACON SAUSAGE

If you are among those fortunate enough to have venison available, try this tasty sausage.

1 pound venison meat	2 teaspoons juniper berries
1 pound pork shoulder	1 teaspoon summer savory
¾ cup dry red wine	½ teaspoon hot paprika
¼ pound bacon	½ teaspoon thyme
¼ pound pork fat	50 inches natural pork
Ice cubes	casings
2 teaspoons coarse salt	

Dice venison and pork meat. Cover with red wine; let marinate in refrigerator overnight. Drain. Discard wine; dry meat.

Grind venison, pork, bacon, and fat twice using the large hole plate on grinder. Add ice cubes during grinding to keep meats cold and clear grinder. Mix salt and spices in a small bowl. Add to meat mixture; mix thoroughly. Refrigerate.

Prepare casings according to instructions. (See Index.)

Sauté a small amount of sausage in a lightly oiled frying pan until thoroughly cooked. Taste and adjust seasonings, if desired.

Stuff sausage into casings according to manufacturer's instructions that accompany grinder or use hand stuffing funnel. Do not overstuff. Refrigerate sausage uncovered at least 12 hours, turning once during that period.

To serve, poach sausage gently in water to cover, about 5 minutes. Drain and dry. Sauté sausage in a lightly oiled frying pan until brown and thoroughly cooked.

Sausage can be refrigerated for several days or frozen for longer periods.

Makes 2½ pounds.

COMMERCIAL
SAUSAGE

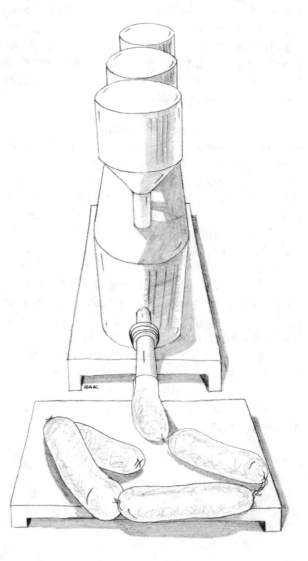

Chapter 7

Commercial production of sausage is, in many ways, similar to home production. There are, of course, some differences due largely to the quantity and types of sausage being made.

At a small, quality-sausage producer's plant, the first noticeable difference is in the parking lot, where a space is reserved for the inspector from the United States Department of Agriculture. The inspector spends half a day here in this plant, watching over all phases of the operation to make certain the ingredients are approved and safe, and that the process adheres to mandatory government regulations. At larger plants, there may be many inspectors who spend all of their time on the premises.

Inside, the plant is spotless from the small consumer sales area near the front door to the packaging areas upstairs. Outside the offices, the employees wear white coats and white hard hats. Visitors—though there are few because of public health considerations—are also required to don a white coat.

In many ways, the plant is like a multiroomed kitchen with separate compartments or stations for various operations and with machinery sized to meet the needs of the processor.

In the initial processing room, commercial grinders and scales look like grown-up kin of our home models. A combination mixer-grinder resembles a giant bowl with cutting knives and is capable of both coarse grinding and mixing.

The spice room is filled with the exotic aroma of seasonings in tightly covered individual containers the size of 50-gallon drums. The proper proportion of each spice is weighed on nearby scales and then the preblended seasonings are placed in brown paper bags, designated for a particular sausage type (as SS denotes Summer Sausage, for example) and shelved for use in the next day's production schedule.

Behind the doors of the smokehouse are hanging racks of sausages soaking up the distinctive flavor of the hardwood smoke, some of which curls out from under the doors and assails the eyes of those not used to it. Here the internal temperature of both the smokehouse and the sausage is carefully monitored to assure a constant proper climate.

Opposite the smokehouse are the water baths, large metal cabinets where more racks of hanging sausages are precooked to a temperature of 185 degrees Fahrenheit.

In another area, employees operate a stuffer which propels sausages along a conveyor belt. Nearby, sausages are packaged and labeled before undergoing a water bath to shrink the packaging around them.

A cold room contains racks of the finished products—fresh bratwursts, which an employee will take home to supper as a fringe benefit, summer sausages still needing their water bath to wrinkle the casings, precooked brats almost white in color as opposed to the fresh brats which are reddish, foot-long beef sticks, and some precooked breakfast links.

In larger plants, continuous systems will make wieners, while other systems will smoke, cook, and chill larger products in one nonstop operation. There are emulsion mills, extruders, various types of stuffers, casing peelers, smokehouses, linkers, conveyor packaging systems, and smoke generating equipment.

Computers, too, are being used to reduce the costs of the operation and ensure uniform, standardized products.

The equipment and the methods vary from processor to processor and, though the recipes are basically the same, each has subtle variations in order to appeal to the consumer. What most of them have in common, though, is the use of chemical additives necessary to preserve and protect the product during shipping and shelf life.

Commercial sausage labels, and indeed labels of most processed food, demand as much a knowledge of edibles as they do of chemistry. The Code of Federal Regulations (CFR), a multivolume guide available in most libraries, lists a nine-page

usage chart of approved food additives, ranging from simple
sugar to those with long, barely pronounceable chemical names
(See CFR Title 9, Chap. III, section 318.7).

A glance at a sausage label often reveals among the meat, salt,
and flavorings, such things as dextrose, sodium erythorbate,
sodium nitrite, citric acid, propyl gallate, BHT, and BHA.

The presence of additives in processed food has created con-
cern among consumers. But their use, which is regulated by the
federal government, is likely to continue because they serve
specific purposes.

Sodium nitrite in sausage, for instance, is a curing agent and
a color enhancer, which provides the red and pink hues so
prevalent in commercial products. More importantly, it is also a
powerful deterrent to the growth of botulism bacteria, a deadly
toxin which develops in spoiled food.

Flavoring agents, which help develop or enhance flavor, include harmless bacteria starters of the acidophilus type, lactic
acid starter, or a culture of *Pediococcus cere visiae* used in dry
sausage, pork roll, Lebanon bologna, cervelat, and salami.

Corn syrup solids, corn syrup, and glucose syrup are used to
flavor sausage, hamburger, meat loaf, luncheon meat, and
chopped or pressed ham.

Dextrose, also used to flavor sausage, ham, and cured products, is also essential to the fermenting process in the production of dry sausage.

Sorbitol, in addition to flavoring, facilitates casing removal,
and reduces carmelization and charring. It is used in cooked
sausage labeled frankfurter, frank, furter, wiener, or knockwurst.

The sugars also aid the browning process and mask the salty
taste of products with high salt contents.

BHT (butylated hydroxytoluene), or BHA (butylated hydroxy-
anisole), and propyl gallate belong to a group of antioxidants
and oxygen interceptors which are used to retard rancidity.
They appear in dry sausage, fresh pork sausage, brown and
serve sausages, Italian sausage products, pregrilled beef patties,

and fresh sausage made from pork and beef or beef only.

Natural coloring agents such as alkanet, annatto, carotene cochineal, green chlorophyll, saffron, and turmeric are used to color casings and to brand or mark products.

Artificial sweeteners are synergists which must be used in combination with antioxidants, enhancing their actions. Citric acid increases the effectiveness of antioxidants in dry sausage and monoglyceride citrate does the same in fresh pork sausage.

There are several curing accelerators, to be used only in combinations with curing agents, which hasten the color fixation. Glucone delta lactone is used in cured, comminuted meat or meat food products and in Genoa salami. Sodium acid pyrophosphate is used in frankfurters, wieners, viennas, bologna, garlic bologna, knockwurst, and similar products.

Sodium ascorbate, which improves color preservation during the storage period, is an ingredient in cured pork and beef cuts and in cured comminuted food products. Sodium erythorbate, citric acid, and sodium citrate do the same.

Sausage may also include a binder, which is used to keep the ingredients together and to make the product go farther. These include enzyme (rennet) treated calcium reduced dried skim milk and calcium lactate. Isolated soy protein, sodium caseinate, dried whey, and cereal flours are also used as sausage binders.

Two elements—potassium sorbate and propyl paraben (propyl p-hydroxybenzoate)—are used to retard mold growth in dry sausages.

A cursory reading of the federal regulations (See CFR Title 9, Chap. III, section 319 subsections E, F, and G) also points out some interesting limitations about the fat and water content of commercial sausage.

Uncooked smoked sausage may be seasoned with approved condiments but "it shall not be made with any lot of product which, in the aggregate, contains more than 50 percent trimmable fat; that is, fat which can be removed by thorough practicable trimming and sorting." Water or ice may also be used in an amount "not to exceed three percent of the total ingredients used."

Frankfurters, franks, furters, hot dogs, wieners, viennas, garlic bologna, knackwurst, and similar products can contain no more than thirty percent fat and ten percent water.

Fresh pork sausage is limited to fifty percent fat and three percent water. The limits for fresh beef sausage are thirty percent fat and three percent water.

"Breakfast sausage" can be fifty percent fat and three percent water but Italian sausage products are limited to no more than thirty five percent fat and three percent water.

The principal ingredients in commercially made sausage products must also be listed on the label according to federal regulations. The major ingredient, by weight, must appear first on the list, followed by the other ingredients in descending order.

Additives must also be listed but colors and flavors need not be identified by name. The label therefore can say simply "spice" or "flavorings" but if the coloring agent is artificial that fact must be stated.

In 1974, the United States Department of Agriculture decreed that the terms hot dogs, franks, furters, frankfurters, and wieners all identified the same product. The labeling requirements were also refined.

Since all cooked sausages include seasonings, water, and curing ingredients, words like "all meat" and "pure beef" were banned as misleading. Three new labeling categories were set up. (See Figure 7-1 on page 104).

The first covers products which formerly were called "all meat" or something similar. They now are simply designated by name and they must be made only from skeletal muscle meat— the meat derived from a primal part of the carcass. If they are made from meat from only one species of animal they may be termed, for example, "beef frankfurters."

The second category of labeling covers cooked sausages with "variety meats"—hearts, tripe, tongue, and other edible byproducts, along with the skeletal muscle meat. The label on these products must clearly state that they are, for example, "franks with byproducts" or "franks with variety meats."

When binders, such as nonfat dry milk and soy flour, are present in the product, it falls into the third category and its label must clearly reflect the addition of these ingredients. The labels will say, for example, "franks with byproducts, nonfat dry milk added" or "beef franks, soy flour added."

The same regulations apply to the listing of all ingredients in the product—with the major ingredient, by weight, listed first, and the others following in descending order.

FIGURE 7-1: USDA Labeling Categories

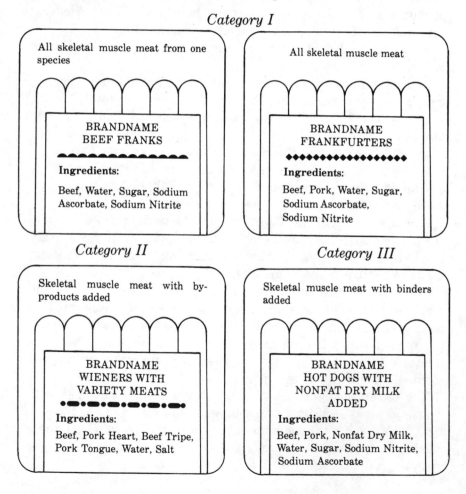

Category I

All skeletal muscle meat from one species

BRANDNAME
BEEF FRANKS

Ingredients:

Beef, Water, Sugar, Sodium Ascorbate, Sodium Nitrite

All skeletal muscle meat

BRANDNAME
FRANKFURTERS

Ingredients:

Beef, Pork, Water, Sugar, Sodium Ascorbate, Sodium Nitrite

Category II

Skeletal muscle meat with by-products added

BRANDNAME
WIENERS WITH
VARIETY MEATS

Ingredients:

Beef, Pork Heart, Beef Tripe, Pork Tongue, Water, Salt

Category III

Skeletal muscle meat with binders added

BRANDNAME
HOT DOGS WITH
NONFAT DRY MILK
ADDED

Ingredients:

Beef, Pork, Nonfat Dry Milk, Water, Sugar, Sodium Nitrite, Sodium Ascorbate

In June, 1978, the federal government approved the use of Mechanically Processed (Species) Product—MP(S)P—in certain processed red meat products including sausage, frankfurters, and canned spaghetti with meat sauce.

MP(S)P is produced by breaking up bones from which most of the meat has been removed by traditional hand means, then using high pressure to push the resultant mass against a fine sieve. MP(S)P is composed of the soft tissue and a small amount of bone that passes through the sieve. The remaining bone is discarded.

The use of MP(S)P is limited to twenty percent of the meat portion of the product and its presence must be clearly indicated. Currently, labels must carry the phrase, "With Mechanically Processed (Species) Product," in letters at least one-half the size of the product name. In addition, the presence of powdered bone also must be noted on the front label with the phrase "contains up to __ percent powdered bone" in letters one-fourth the size of the product name. Proposals to alter the labeling requirements are now under consideration.

The presence of MP(S)P must also be included in the ingredient listing portion of the label.

Finally, the federal regulations require that all labels carry the name of the product, its net weight, and the name and place of business of the distributor, packer, or manufacturer.

GLOSSARY OF SAUSAGES

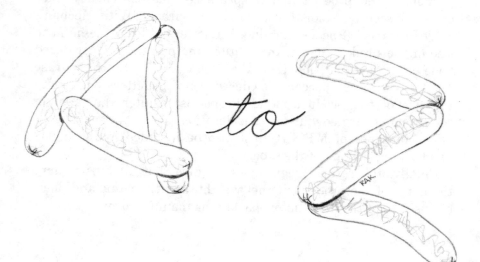

Chapter 8

The wide array of sausages dazzles shoppers who pop into the supermarket to buy edibles for Sunday breakfast, lunchtime sandwich fixings, dinner, and even cocktail snacks or appetizers.

Among the varieties are sausages with widely divergent tastes and others whose differences are hardly discernible. Some are sold in the meat department, some at the delicatessen counter, and still others turn up in the refrigerated case with the cold meat loaf products and the canned hams.

The challenge is to figure out which commercial sausage is which and to choose those which satisfy our particular palates, dietary needs, and ethnic preferences.

The American Meat Institute has provided the following descriptions for many popular sausage varieties. The list also includes those products defined as cooked meat specialties because they fit the definition of sausage in that they are chopped, seasoned meats. Prepared meats, while not technically sausages, are also included because they are meats which have undergone some form of processing.

FRESH SAUSAGE

Bockwurst—A highly perishable sausage, bockwurst is primarily veal, with some pork, and includes milk, eggs, chives, and parsley. The seasonings are similar to those in frankfurters—garlic, coriander, mustard, nutmeg, salt, sugar, and pepper—though bockwurst may have additional seasonings.

Bratwurst—A popular, highly seasoned sausage, bratwurst is made with all pork or with a pork and veal mixture.

Pork sausage—A pure pork product with light seasoning, generally black pepper, nutmeg, and sage, pork sausage is an all-time breakfast favorite.

Pork sausage, country style—This product is almost the same as the one above, except that the pork is more coarsely ground. It is often found in bulk form rather than encased.

Pork sausage, Italian style—Another all-pork product that is highly spiced, Italian-style pork sausage is a popular topping for pizza and is equally tasty in sandwiches or spaghetti sauce.

Salsiccia—This highly seasoned Italian sausage is made with finely ground pork.

Thuringer style—Seasoned like pork sausage, this product consists primarily of ground pork, though sometimes veal and beef may be included.

Weisswurst—A highly perishable, lightly seasoned German creation of pork and veal, its name means "white sausage" in English.

UNCOOKED, SMOKED SAUSAGE

Linguisa—This Portuguese sausage is a blend of coarsely ground pork spiced with garlic, cinnamon, and cumin, which is then cured in a vinegar pickling solution before stuffing and smoking.

Longanzia—This is another name for Linguisa sausage.

Mettwurst—A smooth, spreadable, lightly spiced German sausage, mettwurst is made with cured beef and pork spiced with coriander, allspice, ginger, and mustard.

Polish sausage—Often called Kielbasa (the Polish word for sausage), this coarsely ground lean pork and beef product is highly seasoned with garlic and is traditional fare at most Polish festive dinners.

Pork sausage, smoked country style—A lightly seasoned cousin of the other pork sausages, this product differs in that the meat has first been mildly cured and the sausage is smoked after stuffing.

COOKED SAUSAGE

Blood sausage—Beef blood is a primary ingredient· in this product, which is sometimes called kiska or blutwurst. It also includes diced, cooked pork fat, finely ground cooked pork meat, or beef and pork meat, and gelatinous materials to bind the ingredients together.

Blood and tongue sausage—True to its name, this product must include both ingredients, though they sometimes are ground together. Often, too, the strips of lamb and pork tongue are inserted in the center of the blood sausage.

Braunschweiger—A variation of the popular liver sausage, braunschweiger has either been smoked after cooking or has smoked meats, such as bacon, included in its ingredients.

Liver cheese—Almost the same product as liver sausage, liver cheese is molded into a square loaf and is identifiable by its border of white fat.

Liver loaf—This is another name for liver cheese.

Liver sausage—A favorite sandwich filler, this mildly seasoned product includes finely ground pork and livers and onions.

Thuringer—While sometimes marketed as a fresh sausage, thuringer may be found in cooked form too.

The following four products, though called salamis, are actually cooked sausages. All must be kept under refrigeration.

Beerwurst or beer salami—A product of Germany, beerwurst is made of ground beef and pork, moistened with beer, and combined with spices which include garlic. It is then stuffed into casings, cooked at high temperatures, and smoked.

Cooked salami—This product has a softer texture than either dry sausage varieties and it may also be air dried for a short period of time. The primary ingredients are spices blended with cured fresh meats which are then stuffed into casings and cooked at high temperatures in the smokehouse.

Cotto salami—A soft-textured cooked sausage, cotto salami has whole peppercorns and may be both cooked and smoked.

Kosher salami—Rabbinical approval of the meat and its processing is necessary for this all-beef product which also includes nutmeg, coriander, and mustard in addition to the standard seasonings.

COOKED, SMOKED SAUSAGE

Berliner-style sausage—Lightly seasoned with only sugar and salt, this sausage is made of mildly cured, finely chopped beef combined with coarsely ground, cured pork.

Bologna—One of the most popular of all sausages, bologna is very finely ground cured beef and pork seasoned much like frankfurters.

Beef bologna—An all-beef product, this sausage has a distinct garlic taste.

Chub bologna—This beef and pork sausage is smoother in texture than plain bologna and has bacon added to it.

Ham-style bologna—Large cubes of ham are a principal ingredient in this high-quality bologna variation.

Boterhamworst—A sausage of Dutch origin, this product consists of finely chopped veal and pork, coarsely ground pork fat, and seasonings.

Frankfurter—Beef, or beef and pork, is used to make this popular sausage. The seasoned meat is cured, smoked and cooked. Some of the seasonings include salt, sugar, mustard, pepper, garlic, nutmeg, and coriander.

Garlic sausage—This is another name for knackwurst.

Knackwurst—Often called a German hot dog, knackwurst is very much like a frankfurter but generally has more garlic and is a bit larger in size.

Knoblauch—This term is also used for knackwurst.

Mortadella, German style—Actually a finely chopped bologna of high quality, the ingredients in this sausage include pistachio nuts and chunks of pork fat.

New England-style sausage—Cured lean pork is coarsely chopped for this product, which is much like Berliner-style sausage.

Smokies or smoked links—Seasoned with black pepper, smokies are a coarsely ground beef and pork link sausage.

Vienna sausage—The product is very similar to frankfurters though the term now is generally used to designate the small sausages canned in water or brine for use as appetizers.

Wiener—The wiener was originally made in a size similar to a frankfurter but with seasonings geared to the Viennese taste. The term is now used interchangeably with frankfurter, hot dog, and red hot.

DRY SAUSAGE—DRY

Chorizo—A highly spiced Spanish sausage, chorizos are made of coarsely ground pork which is smoked after stuffing.

Frizzes—A highly seasoned sausage of coarsely ground cured lean pork and a small amount of cured lean beef, frizzes come in two varieties—one which includes hot spices and another seasoned with sweet spices.

Lola—This is a mildly seasoned Italian sausage made with pork and seasoned with garlic.

Lolita—Sure enough, this is a small lola sausage!

Lyons—Lyons sausage originated in the French town of the same name and is made of pork meat, small pieces of diced pork fat, and garlic.

Pepperoni—The hot spicy flavor of this Italian sausage comes from red pepper added to the other seasonings and coarsely ground beef and pork. Pepperoni is a favorite pizza topping.

Salami—The term salami is mentioned in Greek literature before the birth of Christ, which leads to the belief that salami may have originated in the Mediterranean community of Salamis. The term salami as we know it designates a family of dry sausages made primarily of coarsely ground cured lean pork, finely ground cured beef, and seasonings.

Alesandri salami—Born in America, this product is an Italian-style salami, seasoned with garlic and mustard.

Alpino salami—This is also an Italian-style salami of American origin.

Arles salami—Much like Milano salami, this French creation is made of coarsely ground, rather than finely ground, meat.

Calabrese salami—Hot peppers spice up this generally all-pork product, which originated in Italy.

Easter Nola—A little known Italian dry sausage, Easter Nola is made of coarsely ground pork mildly seasoned with various spices including garlic and black pepper.

Genoa salami—An Italian-type salami which originated in the city of the same name, Genoa salami is usually an all-pork product, though it may contain a small amount of beef.

German salami—This product is not as flavorful as Italian-style salami, though it does contain garlic among its seasonings and it is generally smoked longer than those of Italian origin.

Hungarian salami—A subtle variation of German salami, the Hungarian creation also contains garlic and undergoes heavy smoking.

Italian salami—The term is often used in a generic sense to identify any salami of Italian origin. In other cases, the particular Italian salami will be designated by the city, town, or region of its creation, such as Milan, Genoa, or Sicily. At any rate, the Italian salamis contain a variety of spices but almost always include garlic. They may be moistened with wine, usually red wine, or with grape juice.

Milano salami—A favorite among the Italian-style salamis, the Milano variety is primarily pork with a small amount of finely gound beef added.

Sicilian salami—An Italian-style variety which originated in Sicily.

DRY SAUSAGE—SEMI-DRY

Cervelat—Like the term salami, "cervelat" has come to be used in the generic sense to designate a family of semi-dry mildly seasoned sausages which are also smoked. Another term now widely used to designate this type of sausage is "summer sausage," though that term in proper usage refers to all dry sausages.

Farmer cervelat—A mildly seasoned, garlic-less sausage, farmer cervelat is made of equal parts beef and pork which are coarsely ground, cured, and dried.

Göttinger cervelat—A high quality, distinctively seasoned hard cervelat, Göttinger's primary meats are pork and beef.

Göteborg cervelat—Named after the Swedish community of Göteborg where it originated, this cervelat is a heavily smoked, slightly salty product of coarsely ground pork and beef. It includes cardamom among its spices, which gives it a sweet flavor.

Gothaer cervelat—A German creation from the city of Gotha, Gothaer contains only very lean, finely ground pork which is cured.

Holsteiner cervelat—A product very much like farmer cervelat, Holsteiner can be identified by its ring-shaped packaging.

Land Jaeger cervelat—A heavily smoked, beef and pork product, this Swiss creation has a black, wrinkled look and is stuffed into frankfurter-size casings which are then flattened out and smoked.

Thuringer cervelat—This mildly spiced, tangy flavored favorite can be made of beef with either ham or pork fat.

Lebanon bologna—This sour, pungent, dark product originated in Lebanon, Pennsylvania, and is made of coarsely ground beef and is heavily smoked.

Mortadella—A delicately spiced Italian sausage, mortadella contains chopped cured pork and beef with pieces of pork fat added. Garlic and anise are among its seasonings and it is smoked at high temperatures and then air dried.

Summer sausage—This is not a product but a term which properly refers to all dry sausages. It is however used mostly to designate the mildly seasoned, soft cervelats.

COOKED MEAT SPECIALTIES

Sliced beef—A product made from boneless beef which has been chopped, cooked, smoked, and sliced. It is not dehydrated and thus is moist and more perishable than dried beef.

Jellied beef loaf—Usually cooked in a roll or a loaf, this cooked beef is shredded and molded in gelatin. Other varieties include jellied tongue, corned beef, and veal loaf.

Jellied corned beef loaf—Similar to jellied beef loaf, this product is made from precooked lean corned beef instead of regular beef.

Deviled ham—Popular as a sandwich spread, deviled ham is made from whole hams which have been finely ground and seasoned.

Chopped ham—A product with the taste and color of ham, this firm loaf is made from cured pork which has been ground, chopped, or cubed.

Ham and cheese loaf—This is much like chopped ham but has chunks of firm cheese added to it.

Head cheese—A gelatin loaf made from the chopped, cured meats of the animal's head.

Honey loaf—As its name implies, the seasonings in this beef and pork product, which is similar to bologna and frankfurters, include honey. Sometimes it also includes pickles or pimientos.

Luncheon meat—A very broad term that encompasses a family of cooked meat specialties, it can also denote a single product as well. This is made of seasoned chopped pork, beef, or ham, or combinations of meats, and is available in loaf, canned, or sliced forms.

Macaroni and cheese loaf—The basis of this product is finely ground pork and beef to which macaroni and cheddar cheese have been added.

Minced luncheon meat—A variation of luncheon meat, this product is made of cured lean pork and beef trimmings which have been finely ground and seasoned.

Old-fashioned loaf—A firm loaf of lean pork blended with some beef for flavor and firmness.

Olive loaf—A fine-textured mixture of lean pork and beef which is blended with seasonings and whole stuffed olives.

Pepper loaf—A loaf made of pressed beef and pork and cracked peppercorns.

Pickle and pimiento loaf—Sweet pickles and pimientos are added to this finely chopped lean pork and beef product.

Scrapple—An old-time favorite, scrapple is made of cooked ground pork and cornmeal, though it may include small amounts of other flours.

Souse or Sülz—A vinegar-pickle gives this product a sweet-sour taste which is similar to head cheese. It can also have dill pickles, bay leaves, and sweet red peppers.

Veal loaf—Some pork may be added to this loaf but it is primarily veal meat ground, seasoned and jellied.

PREPARED MEAT PRODUCTS

Beef, dried or "chipped"—A thinly sliced, long-cured product made from beef round, chipped beef is cured, smoked, and dehydrated.

Cappicola Made from boneless pork shoulder butt, Cappicola originated in Italy and is seasoned with ground peppers, either hot or sweet, paprika, salt, and sugar. It is mildly cured and air dried.

Ham, cooked—Often called "boiled" ham, this popular product is cured, molded, and fully cooked, generally by steam or water.

Pastrami—A favorite sandwich item, pastrami is made from flat pieces of lean beef, dry-cured, rubbed with a spicy paste and smoked.

Prosciutto—Made of flattened pieces of dry-cured ham which have been rubbed with spices, prosciutto is often served as an antipasto or with melon.

Tongue, cooked—Lamb, pork, and veal tongues are generally cured and they can be smoked as well. They are available either canned or in plastic packages. Beef tongues can be purchased jellied, whole, or in slices for use in sandwiches.

SUGGESTIONS

Chapter 9

COOKING SAUSAGE

Unlike many cuts of meat which must be cooked a certain way to enhance their flavor and tenderness, sausage is a much more versatile product. Its preparation method depends largely on personal preference, the occasion, and the balance of the menu.

Fresh sausage and uncooked, smoked sausages must be thoroughly cooked before eating. The internal temperature should reach 155 degrees F. before the product can be eaten.

In cooking sausage, as well as all other foods, it is important to remember the carry-over factor. While waiting to be served, all cooked foods continue to cook even though they have been removed from the heat source. This carry-over factor exists because the internal temperature of the food decreases slowly; it cannot go immediately from hot to cold. Fine pork sausage must be cooked thoroughly but it should not be overcooked and dried out. If its internal temperature is 155 degrees F., or if the interior color is gray rather than pink, the cooking process is complete.

Sausages are also fairly fragile and should be handled gently during the cooking process. Patties should be turned with a spatula, while links will survive better if handled with tongs. Using a fork on link sausage only pierces the casings and allows the flavorful juices to escape. However, with some commercial sausages, piercing may be necessary to release some of the fat, since the fat-to-lean ratio is higher than in our recipes.

The Cooking Methods for Sausage

Bake: Arrange sausages on a rack in either a shallow baking pan or on a baking sheet that has four sides. The oven temperature should be 400 degrees F. and the patties or links should bake about 15 to 20 minutes, depending on their thickness.

Broil: Place the sausage patties or links on a broiler pan about three inches from the heat source. Turn them and watch closely because it will only take a few minutes per side to broil the sausages completely.

Grill: Fresh sausages can be blanched before grilling to prevent the casings from bursting, which allows the juices to escape, during high heat grilling. To blanch sausage, place the links in a pan of water and heat the water to a boil. Remove the pan from the heat and allow it to stand for five or ten minutes. Remove the sausages from the water and place them on the grill over moderately hot coals. The cooking time depends on the heat of the coals and the sausage's internal temperature should be tested before serving.

Pan Broil or Saute: Sausage should be browned in a heavy pan which contains a small amount of fat. Turn them to achieve even browning and test the internal temperature for doneness before serving.

Simmer: Place fully cooked sausages in boiling water, beer, wine, a soft beverage, or fruit juice. Cover the pan and simmer five to ten minutes until thoroughly heated.

STORING SAUSAGE

Sausage, like all food, translates into money in edible form. Homemade sausage is even more valuable because it includes the initial expenditure for the ingredients plus the personal labor which transforms the components into a distinctive dish geared to specific palates.

Those should be reasons enough for properly storing sausage but there is also another vital factor to consider: health.

Improperly kept food is food that harbors the potential for the growth of illness-causing bacteria. Some foods store well; other foods do not and still others will benefit from a short storage period to enhance the seasonings.

To ensure quality, all sausage should be refrigerated at 40 degrees F. or lower. It is particularly important to keep fresh sausage, and those which have been sliced, at low temperatures.

Whole, dry, hard sausages will keep for a relatively long time at "cool room temperature"—about 50 degrees F. However, few homes can be comfortably maintained at that low a temperature, so it is better to refrigerate this group of sausages too.

Hard sausages can be kept in a home where there is a cold, dry storage room. But beware of cedar-lined rooms which can impart a cedar taste to the sausage. Be careful, too, of storing sausage, or any other food, in your garage because of the noxious fumes prevalent there. Crawl spaces are often too moist for safely storing food and it is wiser to depend on your refrigerator.

Fresh sausage will keep several days under proper refrigeration. But bear in mind that the color will change from pink to gray and the flavor will undergo subtle alterations during this time because the spices will weaken or become stronger depending on which ones are present.

Unopened cooked sausages left in their original packaging should refrigerate well for about two weeks.

It is best to use cooked meats and meat specialties within a week after purchase.

Most sausages store well in the freezer for short periods of time but again caution is advised. Certain spices—onion, garlic, cloves, and pepper—will intensify during freezer storage especially when blended with uncooked meat. Other spices—salt and chili powder to name only two—will get weaker.

It is preferable, then, to limit freezer storage of sausage to one month with an absolute maximum storage period of no more than two months at zero degrees F.

Because of the short freezer life, making sausage in large quantities is not recommended. Instead, apppropriate size packages of ground or unground meat for sausage can be stored in the freezer until needed.

SMOKING SAUSAGE

The smoking process itself has little preservative action; it is the dry salt or the soaking in salt solution which cures the product. Because brining in either form defeats our purpose in making sausage in the first place—to eliminate additives and preservatives which may be detrimental to one's health—we do not smoke sausage, or anything else, to *preserve* it.

Like many others, however, we do enjoy the smoke flavor. Smoking fresh sausage or other food does offer another menu variety in the everpresent search for something different to eat.

We have three smokers; two are factory made, come with detailed instructions, and are available on the retail market. The third is homemade (See Equipment, Chapter 3) and using it is an art, not a science, wholly dependent on individual tastes. All three smokers are for flavoring purposes only, in different situations.

Life, being fairly hectic, often compels us to use an electric dry smoker. Nothing is easier than plugging it into an outdoor outlet and after that there is very little monitoring because the element is programmed for low heat. The only problem with this unit is the difficulty in adding more wood during the smoking process. The door is small—about eight inches long and about four inches wide—and not quite adequate for the purpose unless the cook correctly estimates the amount of wood necessary for the somewhat lengthy smoking process.

A slightly different flavor is obtained by using a water smoker. Again, the wood needed for smoke production must be accurately estimated. In order to reach the fire source, the top section of the smoker, which includes the pan filled with hot water, must be completely lifted off the bottom section to add more chips.

Because this smoker is nonelectric it takes more monitoring than the dry smoker in order to maintain both the wood and charcoal levels.

The smoker we've had the most fun with is the one we created ourselves from the old whiskey barrel.

Further processing of fresh sausage by smoking or drying is an art unto itself and one better left to professional sausage makers because improperly smoked or dried sausage can cause serious health problems.

It is important, then, to remember that we smoke sausage for flavor and flavor only and that the cooking process is always completed on our kitchen stove. The sausage then is tested with an instant-registering microwave thermometer to guarantee the proper internal temperature—155 degrees F.—before serving.

To begin our smoking operation, the bottom of the fire pit is lined with aluminum foil because it provides easy removal of the ash once the smoking process is complete. Excess ash, depending on the location of the barrel itself, can be blown onto the sausages if it builds up in the fire pit. Though we have had little problems of this sort, because of our six-foot trench, smoke-houses placed directly above the fire pit will run a greater chance of producing ash-blown food.

We use charcoal as the fire base for several reasons: it is readily available, cheaper than hardwood, easier to maintain than a wood fire, and smokeless. We also use an electric fire starter rather than starter fluid, which might impart a peculiar taste to the sausage.

Because our smoking process is one of slow, partial cooking and drying, a high flame is neither advantageous nor necessary. White-hot coals are best and about ten of them should suffice at the onset of the smoking process. Higher heat at the beginning of the operation will reduce the moisture after which the temperature can be reduced. We maintain a temperature of about 140 degrees F. in our smoker and consider ours a hot smoking operation which also partially, and only partially, cooks the sausage. Cold smoking is done at lower temperatures, usually below 90 degrees F. and has little cooking capability.

The fire is regulated by raising the sheet metal so that it is two or three inches off the ground on the side facing the wind. On a calm day, a larger opening may be needed and conversely, on a windy day the opening may have to be tamped down to prevent a roaring blaze from developing.

The flavor of the smoked product depends upon the type of hardwood used to produce the smoke. This is largely a matter of personal preference. Experimentation with a number of different hardwoods—apple, willow, hickory, maple, birch, oak, cherry—will provide an almost endless array of distinctive smoked meals.

Soft woods such as pine, cedar, and spruce should not be used because they are highly resinous and produce a bitter taste in the food being smoked.

Small pieces of wood, or wood chips, are easier to handle and will burn better than large logs. Soaking them in water for several hours, or overnight, will increase the smoke they produce when placed on the fire and will also help contain the flame.

Huge amounts of smoke are not necessary—small wisps lend a delicate smoky flavor to the sausage and great clouds of smoke will contribute a heavy smoked flavor. Smoke that is just visible escaping from the top of our smoker imparts about the right taste for us and it does not cloud up the neighborhood or offend those who live nearby. As in the types of wood to be used, the amount of smoke is a matter of personal preference based on experimentation.

Sausages smoke best if they are dry when they are hung in the smoker. Moisture on the outside of them may attract ash and may prevent them from taking on a smoky color. Homemade sausage, though, will never resemble commercial sausages because they lack the chemical additives and preservatives which are often color enhancers.

The sausages should be hung over the smoker sticks with sufficient space between them so they do not touch each other. This allows the smoke to flow around all sides of the product. Once the sausages are in place, the top of the barrel is placed on the smoker and the process begins.

The temperature in the smoker should be monitored every 15 to 20 minutes and the fire inspected to make certain there are still enough burning coals and wood chips to produce the desired heat and amount of smoke.

Sausage can be left in the smoker as long as desirable, so long as the fire is maintained. We often leave sausage to smoke for about four hours and then complete the cooking process in the kitchen to guarantee an internal temperature of at least 155 degrees F.

MENU IDEAS

Chapter 10

Sausage paired with eggs is an American breakfast staple, but sausage, especially homemade sausage, should not be limited to the early morning hours. You can tuck it into a biscuit and have a sausage sandwich for lunch or crumble it into a Yorkshire Pudding batter for a unique dinner treat. You can grill sausage for outdoor parties, make it into hors d'oeuvres, serve it as a late evening snack, or use it on pizza for the kids.

SERVING SAUSAGE

Serving Portions

Your serving portions may differ from the number given in the recipe depending on the age and appetite of the people you are serving, time of day, and other dishes served at the meal. Teenagers may eat two portions each while young children may eat less than a full share. A meal accompanied by vegetables, salad, and dessert will, of course, extend the meat servings. These factors should be considered when preparing menus.

Sausage Flexibility

We have not often specified which type of sausage should be used in these servings suggestions. If we specify a sausage other than the one you have on hand you might not try the menu idea. We urge you to be flexible in using sausage and the serving suggestions. The kind of sausage is not really important, anyway, unless the one you have selected would substantially alter the flavor of the finished dish.

Salt

The use of salt in the following menu ideas has either been

eliminated or listed "to taste." With medical research warning us about the dangers of using too much salt, we suggest you use it sparingly. Keep in mind that the sausage has salt in it and salt may also have been added to other ingredients during the processing.

Instant Flour

A blend of hard and soft wheats, "instant flour" is produced by a process of agglomeration which creates noncohesive clusters of similar-size flour particles. Its texture is akin to the texture of salt and it mixes readily with hot or cold liquids without lumping. The only brand we've found on the market is Gold Medal Wondra® made by General Mills—an all-pourpose flour which contains no chemical additives and can be substituted in equal amounts for standard flour.

The following menu ideas are only some of the many ways sausage can be incorporated into your daily meal planning. We hope you'll enjoy them and that they will become the basis for your own collection of sausage menus.

APPLE FRITTERS

The batter is guaranteed to stay on these delicious Apple Fritters.

4 Golden Delicious or Rome
   Beauty apples
1 tablespoon lemon juice
1 egg
1 egg white
About ½ cup water

1 cup pancake mix
¼ cup cornstarch
Vegetable oil
⅓ cup sugar mixed with 1
   teaspoon cinnamon

Pare apples; slice into thick rounds. Place apples in water to cover to which lemon juice has been added, in a large bowl.

Beat egg and egg white in a bowl until thoroughly mixed. Add ½ cup water; blend. Add pancake mix and cornstarch to egg mixture; mix well, adding more water if necessary to make a thicker batter than used for pancakes. Batter will thicken within minutes if cooking is delayed.

Drain apples well.

Heat electric frying pan, which has been covered with ¼ inch of vegetable oil, until hot, 375°. Dip apple rounds in batter. Cook in frying pan until brown, turning once during cooking period.

Place cooked fritters on paper toweling. Keep fritters warm until all have been cooked. Sprinkle fritters with cinnamon-sugar mixture or serve with honey or warm syrup, accompanied by cooked, mildly seasoned sausage.

Makes 12 fritters.

APPLE PANCAKES WITH SAUSAGE

This is a good way to have a complete breakfast in a pancake. Buttermilk pancakes are always best, and dry buttermilk is now available in supermarkets. Prepare the pancake batter of your choice or use the following recipe:

1 large egg
1¼ cups buttermilk or
   reconstituted dry
   buttermilk
1 tablespoon sugar
1 cup all-purpose flour
1 teaspoon baking powder

½ teaspoon baking soda
½ teaspoon salt
½ pound loose breakfast
   sausage, cooked and
   drained
½ cup grated apple

Beat egg in a large bowl; add buttermilk and sugar. Mix flour, baking powder, baking soda, and salt in a small bowl. Add to egg mixture; mix well. (Batter may appear lumpy.) Add sausage and apple. Batter may need to be adjusted; add more liquid if too thick.

Heat a greased frying pan to 350° or until water dropped on pan sizzles. Pour batter into frying pan or griddle to make 4-inch pancakes. Turn pancakes only once. Serve immediately with warm syrup or honey.

Makes about 12 4-inch pancakes.

BAKED BEANS AND SAUSAGE CASSEROLE

Bertie's sister Rae Feil frequently serves this favorite dinner to her husband and eight children. You will do the same, especially since this savory dish can be made ahead and then just heated.

1 pound white beans
1 teaspoon salt
1 tablespoon prepared
   mustard
1 cup dark brown sugar
2 tablespoons molasses

¼ cup catsup
¼ cup minced onion
½ cup bean water
1 pound sausage of your
   choice, with no
   predominant seasoning

Cover beans with water in a 4-quart saucepan or Dutch oven. Heat beans to boiling. Remove from heat; cover and let soak 1 hour. Drain and discard water; rinse beans. Cover again with water; add salt. Heat beans to boiling; reduce heat. Simmer beans until tender, but not overcooked, 35 to 50 minutes. Drain and reserve bean water.

Heat oven to 350°. Combine beans, mustard, brown sugar, molasses, catsup, onions, and ½ cup bean water in a baking dish; mix well. Bake beans for 45 minutes.

While beans are baking, simmer sausage in casing in water to cover, 10 to 15 minutes. Drain. Place sausage on top of beans; bake beans 15 to 25 minutes longer.

Remove casserole from oven; cool 10 minutes before serving or cool and then reheat for later serving.

Makes 6 servings.

BAKED POTATOES WITH SAUSAGE

Each of these baked potatoes with sausage is a meal in itself. There is no need for butter, gravy, or sour cream, since sausage imparts a delectable flavor to the potatoes.

**6 baking potatoes, skins
    scrubbed
1 pound sausage meat or
    links of your choice**

Heat oven to 400°. Bake potatoes until done, about 45 minutes.

About 20 minutes before potatoes are done, bake sausage in a baking dish until brown but not dry. Remove sausage from dish, drain.

Slit potato tops with a fork; squeeze sides. Place sausage on top. Serve immediately.

Makes 6 servings.

BISCUITS

These are dandy, cut as large as a roll, and used to make a sausage sandwich. What could be tastier than these big morsels for breakfast? Or for lunch and for dinner served with soup and salad? Made in miniature size, biscuits are wonderful hors d'oeuvres, too.

2½ cups all-purpose flour
1 tablespoon baking
   powder
½ teaspoon salt
½ cup cold shortening or
   margarine

About ¾ cup milk
Egg white, beaten, if
   desired
Sesame or poppy seed, if
   desired

Heat oven to 450°. Mix flour, baking powder, and salt in a large bowl. Using pastry blender (or fingers if the shortening is refrigerator cold), cut in fat until mixture is the consistency of small peas. Add milk; stir gently with a rubber spatula until a soft dough forms.

Place dough on a lightly floured surface; knead gently 10 to 12 times until dough forms a ball and is not sticky. Roll dough to less than ½ inch thickness and cut with a 3 to 4 inch cutter. (Using a smooth surface cutting can opener, remove both ends of tuna fish can. Wash in detergent and baking soda and use as cutter.)

Place biscuits ½ inch apart on ungreased baking sheet. (If a crusty side is desired, place about 1 inch apart.) Biscuits can be glazed with beaten egg white and sprinkled with sesame seed or poppy seed. Bake biscuits 8 to 10 minutes. Remove from oven. Serve immediately.

Note: To make a sausage sandwich using biscuits, prepare 2 pounds of any country roll-type sausage or Roundettes (see Index). Sauté sausage in a lightly oiled frying pan until brown (pork sausage must be cooked thoroughly). Drain.

Split baked biscuits; place sausage on biscuits; serve immediately.

Makes 8 to 10 large biscuits.

CORN SAUSAGE CUSTARD

Not unlike dessert rice pudding, this savory custard is sure to become a favorite. You can also use succotash for a change. This high-in-nutrition meal is ideal for buffet serving or brunch.

1 pound sausage of your choice (preferably with no predominant spice flavor)
½ cup diced onion
¼ cup chopped green pepper (optional)
2 large eggs

Liquid from drained corn plus milk to make 1½ cups
2 tablespoons instant flour
1 12-ounce can whole kernel corn
Salt and white pepper to taste

Generously butter a medium-size casserole dish. Heat oven to 350°.

Sauté sausage in a lightly oiled frying pan until light brown. Drain, reserve. Sauté onion and green pepper in a small amount of sausage fat until soft but not brown. Reserve.

Beat eggs in the buttered casserole dish until blended. Add milk mixture and flour; mix well. Add sausage, onion, green pepper, and corn. Mix well. Add salt and pepper. Place casserole dish uncovered in a larger pan of hot water, so water level reaches about two-thirds of the way up the sides of the casserole dish. Bake about 15 minutes; stir well. Continue to bake, stir again, and cook until custard begins to thicken but is still soft in the center, about 25 minutes. Remove from oven. Cool 10 minutes.

Makes 6 servings.

DOUBLE PORK STEAKS

Purchase a pork shoulder or Boston butt and you will be able to make a tasty sausage and have this delectable and economical meal.

½ pound sausage of your choice
1 celery stalk, finely chopped
1 small onion, finely diced
3 slices firm-textured bread, crusts removed
2 apples, finely diced
2 tablespoons chopped fresh parsley

6 thin pork shoulder steaks
Vegetable oil
1 cup water
2 tablespoons flour (instant-type preferred)
½ teaspoon salt
¼ teaspoon ground black pepper

Sauté sausage meat gently in a lightly oiled frying pan. Add celery and onion; cook until vegetables are soft but not brown.

Crumble bread in a large bowl. Add sausage mixture, apples, and parsley; mix stuffing well.

Preheat oven to 450°. If steaks are not thin, flatten with a food mallet. Divide stuffing on pork steaks. Make bundles and tie with string.

Bake pork steaks uncovered in a lightly oiled iron frying pan or ovenproof baking dish, 15 to 20 minutes. Reduce heat to 350°; cover and bake about 30 minutes longer.

Remove steaks from oven; cut off string. Keep steaks warm. Discard all but 2 tablespoons of fat from baking dish. Mix 1 cup water, the flour, salt, and pepper; add to fat. Cook until thickened. Serve with creamy mashed potatoes or spätzle (see Index) and gravy.

Makes 6 servings.

EMPANADAS PAPAS

These turnovers can be prepared in advance and used for dinner or as a snack, especially for late evenings. At serving time they can be baked or reheated.

1½ cups diced, pared, uncooked potatoes

2 cups chopped green leafy vegetable, such as escarole, endive, or Swiss chard

1 pound chorizo

1 small onion, chopped

1 tomato, diced

Pastry dough (see Index for recipe)

1 egg white, lightly beaten

Blanch potatoes in boiling water 1 or 2 minutes. Drain; reserve. Wilt vegetable in boiling water. Drain; squeeze out excess water.

Sauté loose chorizo in a lightly oiled frying pan until almost cooked. Remove all but 2 tablespoons of fat from pan. Add onion and tomato. Cook until soft. Add potatoes and wilted vegetable; heat thoroughly. Remove from heat; cool.

Prepare pastry dough. Cut out eight to ten 6-inch circles from dough. On each circle, place prepared filling on half the circle. Brush edges with beaten egg white. Fold circles in half; seal with fork tines. Brush tops with egg white.

Heat oven to 400°. Bake empanadas on a baking sheet 15 to 20 minutes or until crust is baked and brown. Serve immediately or cool and refrigerate until time to reheat.

Makes 6 servings.

ENGLISH MUFFINS

Here is a quickie recipe for breadmakers. No oven is needed.

Use any recipe presently used for homemade bread. After the dough has risen to twice its size, lightly flour a bread board. Turn out dough onto board. Sprinkle lightly with flour. Let dough rest 10 minutes if you have "worked" the dough.

Roll out dough to about ¼ inch thickness; cut into circles with a 3-inch round cutter (see Index for making your own cutter). Place circles on a baking sheet sprinkled with cornmeal. Cover and let rise until almost doubled in size.

Heat an electric frying pan or griddle to 350°, or heat a frying pan to medium hot temperature. Cover pan with cornmeal; do not grease. Using a spatula, place English muffins in frying pan and cook about 6 minutes on each side. Turn, using 2 forks. (If you do not have a temperature-controlled pan, test by cooking only 1 muffin to determine degree of heat.) Remove from pan; cool on rack.

To freeze muffins, cool completely. Split each muffin with a fork and place in freezer bag.

One loaf makes 9 muffins.

FARMER'S OMELET

This is a hearty type of omelet—quick and delicious. It's economical, too, made with leftovers.

Leftover boiled potatoes
Sausage links or meat,
    cooked

Eggs, sufficient for people
    to be served, beaten
    with a small quantity of
    water

Specific amounts are not provided as this omelet can be made for 1 or 6 persons, depending on the family, appetite, and time of day.

Sauté potatoes in an oiled frying pan until almost brown. Add sausage; heat thoroughly. Add eggs; cook and stir until omelet reaches desired doneness, allowing for continued cooking before being served.

Alternate method: If no leftover potatoes or sausage are available, cook potatoes in slices or cubes until tender. Drain and cool. Meanwhile, sauté sausage of your choice in a lightly oiled frying pan until brown and cooked. Drain all but 2 tablespoons fat from the pan. Add potatoes; brown. Add eggs. Cook until firm but soft. Serve immediately for breakfast, lunch, or dinner.

FESTIVE MEAT LOAF

For a different type of meat loaf, try this recipe. It is good enough for company. Your selection of sausage will provide a different meat loaf each time. You will enjoy the crusty texture on the outside of the loaf.

½ cup onion, diced
1 pound lean ground beef
1 pound sausage meat
2 eggs, beaten
1 cup tomato sauce (or
   barbecue sauce
   depending on sausage)
1 teaspoon salt

½ teaspoon freshly ground
   black pepper
½ cup firm-textured bread
   crumbs, crusts included
½ cup fresh parsley, minced
4 thin slices ham
3 to 4 slices Swiss cheese

Sauté onion in a lightly oiled frying pan until soft but not brown. (This step will greatly improve the flavor of the meat loaf.)

Mix ground beef, sausage, eggs, ½ cup of the tomato sauce, salt and pepper in a large bowl. Mix well. Add bread crumbs and parsley; mix thoroughly. Place meat mixture on a large sheet of wax paper. With a rolling pin, roll meat mixture into a rectangle about 12 × 16 inches. Place ham slices on meat loaf; top with cheese. Form meat into a roll using wax paper.

Heat oven to 350°. Place meat loaf seam side down on a broiler pan with a rack for draining fat. Bake meat loaf about 50 minutes. Spread with remaining tomato sauce; bake 10 minutes longer.

Remove from oven. Cool meat loaf about 10 minutes. To serve, cut meat loaf into thick slices. Center will appear pink because of ham slices.

Makes 6 servings.

FRIED RICE AND SAUSAGE

This can be a main course, with rice reserved from a previous cooking.

1 pound sausage meat
3 cups cold cooked rice
6 green onions, tops
    included, thinly sliced

1 tablespoon soy sauce
3 eggs, beaten

Sauté sausage in a lightly oiled frying pan. Remove sausage with a slotted spoon; reserve. Add rice and green onions to frying pan. Sauté until thoroughly heated. Remove any excess fat. Add sausage. Stir in soy sauce and eggs, stirring constantly to incorporate eggs. Serve immediately.

Makes 4 to 6 servings.

FRITTATA

The French call them omelettes and the Italians call them *frittata*. Each is different, though both are made with eggs. This recipe is delicious served for brunch. Cooked potatotes may be substituted for the noodles.

½ pound sausage meat,
    Italian or mildly
    seasoned
6 eggs
¼ cup freshly grated
    Parmesan or Romano
    cheese

¼ cup finely chopped
    parsley
¼ cup finely minced onion
3 tablespoons vegetable oil
1½ cups cooked noodles or
    macaroni
Sliced tomatoes

Sauté sausage in a lightly oiled 10-inch frying pan until brown and cooked. Remove sausage from pan; reserve. Discard fat. Wipe pan with paper toweling.

Beat eggs, cheese, and parsley lightly in a medium-sized bowl. Reserve.

Sauté onion in 3 tablespoons oil in frying pan until soft but not brown. Add noodles or macaroni; stir until heated thoroughly. Add crumbled sausage. Pour in egg mixture. Cook over low heat until underside is crisp, about 10 minutes.

Place frying pan under broiler to brown top or turn out on dish and then slide back into frying pan to brown second side. Again, cook until lightly browned. Cut into wedges and serve with sliced tomatoes.

Makes 6 servings.

GREEN VEGETABLE AND SAUSAGE PIZZA

This double-crusted pizza is a favorite of family and guests. The Italians called the dish *pizza verdura*. Serve it at any hour!

Dough for 1 loaf
  Mediterranean Bread
  (see recipe listed in
  Index)
Sausage and Salad
  Vegetables (see recipe
  listed in Index)

1 tablespoon capers
¼ cup cured, ripe olives,
  pitted and sliced .
  (Italian or Greek)
Egg white, beaten

Make shells for a double-crusted pizza by preparing the dough for 1 loaf of Mediterranean Bread.

Divide dough in half. Stretch half the dough as far as possible in a well-oiled, 10-inch pizza pan. Let dough relax until it can easily be made to fit pan. Form remaining dough into piece of the same size.

Make Sausage and Salad Vegetables. Add capers and olives.

Spread sausage-vegetable mixture over dough in pan. Brush edges of dough with egg white. Cover with second piece of dough. Seal edges together tightly. Brush top of dough with vegetable oil. Pierce dough with a fork to allow steam to escape.

Heat oven to 450°. Bake pizza until brown and crusty, 30 to 35 minutes.

Makes 6 servings.

GYRO

Gyro is an increasingly popular "sandwich," which you'll find you will serve often. Don't wait too long to try it.

Tzatzíki Sauce (see Index)
6 large pita breads
Gyro Meat, thinly sliced,
    heated (see Index for
    recipe)

Thinly sliced onions,
    separated into rings
Thinly sliced or finely
    chopped tomatoes

Specified amounts are not provided in this recipe. You will need 1 large pita bread for each serving. The amounts of the remaining ingredients will depend on how generously you choose to serve Gyros.

Make Tzatzíki Sauce.

Heat each pita quickly on both sides in a lightly oiled frying pan. Place gyro meat on pitas. Cover with onions and tomatoes in desired amounts. Add Tzatzíki sauce; roll up pita breads. Serve immediately.

Note: Since pita bread has a pocket, you may prefer to slit each pita about halfway and place the ingredients inside the bread.

Makes 6 servings.

LAYERED CABBAGE CREOLE

This recipe is simpler than stuffing individual cabbage leaves, but equally delicious.

1 medium head of cabbage
(about 2½ pounds)
1½ pounds sausage meat of
your choice
(Sauerkraut Sausage or
Sunday Breakfast
Sausage are good
selections)
1 medium onion, diced
1 clove garlic, finely
minced or pressed

1 cup cooked rice
1 grated carrot
1 8-ounce can tomato sauce
1 egg, beaten
2 tablespoons finely
chopped fresh parsley
½ teaspoon crumbled thyme
Salt and pepper to taste

Remove core from cabbage; separate leaves. Blanch in boiling water about 2 minutes. Drain cabbage; cover with cold water. Drain again; reserve.

Mix remaining ingredients, but use only ¼ cup tomato sauce, in a large bowl. Mix well.

Heat oven to 325°. Place 2 layers of cabbage leaves in a lightly oiled baking dish, 9½ × 11 inches. Spread sausage mixture over leaves to cover. Repeat layers of cabbage and sausage mixture ending with cabbage leaves. Cover baking dish with aluminum foil. Bake for 50 minutes. Remove foil; add remaining tomato sauce. Bake 10 minutes longer. Remove from oven; cool 10 minutes. Cut in squares and serve hot.

Makes 6 servings.

MEDITERRANEAN BREAD

You can call it Italian, Greek, or French, but they all are made with the same basic ingredients. This versatile bread is inexpensive, low in calories, and absolutely delicious.

1 ounce fresh yeast or 2
    packages dry yeast
2 cups water (100° for
    fresh yeast, 110° for
    dry yeast)

2 tablespoons dehydrated
    potato flakes
5 to 6 cups flour (bread
    flour, if available)
1 tablespoon salt

Soften yeast in water in a large bowl. Add potato flakes, 2 cups of the flour, and the salt. Beat with a mixer or with a wooden spoon until thoroughly mixed. Add 3 cups flour. Beat with wooden spoon (only a mixer with a dough hook can accommodate the additional flour). Reserve 1 cup of flour for kneading bread, using only if necessary.

Turn dough out on well-floured board; knead dough until smooth and satiny, adding flour as necessary. (This is a stiff, lean dough and requires considerable kneading to make a fine-textured bread.)

Place dough in a lightly oiled large bowl; rotate dough until covered with oil. Cover dough directly with plastic wrap. Let stand in a warm place (not over 80°) until doubled in bulk, about 1½ hours. (Beware of pilot-lit ovens or stoves for too high a temperature.)

Note: Remaining instructions will be given in individual recipes.

Makes 2 loaves.

OPEN-FACE ENGLISH MUFFIN—SAUSAGE SANDWICH

Fresh-baked English Muffins and sausage—a better sandwich would be hard to find. Served with homemade applesauce or sautéed apple slices, this will be a popular item for breakfast, lunch, or dinner.

6 English Muffins (see
   Index for recipe)
1½ pounds cooked loose
   sausage or thin patties

12 thin slices tomatoes
12 cheese slices

Make English Muffins. Split muffins in half with a fork, not a knife. Toast muffins, if desired.

Place loose sausage or patty on each half. Top with tomato slice. Place muffins under broiler until hot. Remove from oven. Top each muffin with a cheese slice; return to broiler until cheese is melted. Serve immediately.

Makes 6 servings.

PAPRIKA SAUSAGE SAUTÉ

This recipe is ideal for the no-salt or beef sausage. Lamb sausage is excellent and different.

1 pound sausage meat
1 tablespoon sweet paprika
¼ cup chopped onion
¼ cup beef stock or water
   (do not use bouillon cube)

1 8-ounce can tomato sauce
½ cup dairy sour cream
1 tablespoon chopped fresh
   parsley

Lightly brown sausage in a lightly oiled frying pan. Drain all but 2 tablespoons fat. Add paprika and stir. Add onion; cook until soft but not brown. Add stock and tomato sauce. Simmer about 20 minutes.

Place sour cream in a small bowl. Spoon 1 to 2 tablespoons sauce from meat mixture into sour cream. (This will temper the sour cream so it will not curdle.) Pour sour cream mixture into meat mixture; mix and heat thoroughly. Add parsley. Serve over rice or spätzle (see Index).

Makes 4 servings.

PASTITSIO

This classic Greek dish is perfect for family meals and also for parties. It can easily be made ahead and baked at serving time, and can also be reheated or frozen.

1 pound Pastitsio Sausage (see Index for recipe)
½ pound large elbow macaroni or mostaccioli
1 large onion, finely chopped
½ teaspoon salt
¼ teaspoon ground black pepper
⅛ teaspoon ground nutmeg
⅛ teaspoon ground cinnamon
2 tablespoons dry white wine (optional)
½ cup tomato sauce
Custard Sauce (recipe follows)
¼ cup melted butter or margarine
2 eggs, beaten
1¼ cups freshly grated Romano or Parmesan cheese

Cook macaroni in large quantity salted water until tender but not soft. Drain. Rinse in cold water; drain again. Reserve.

Sauté sausage and onion in a lightly oiled large frying pan. Drain fat. Add salt, pepper, nutmeg, and cinnamon. Mix well. Sauté mixture 1 minute. Add wine and tomato sauce; cook 2 or 3 minutes.

Make Custard Sauce.

Heat oven to 350°. Add butter to cooked macaroni; mix well. Add eggs and ¼ cup of the cheese. Stir in sausage mixture. Pour mixture into a buttered baking dish, 9 × 13 inches. Cover with Custard Sauce. Spread remaining 1 cup cheese over custard. Bake for 30 to 35 minutes. Remove from oven. Cover; cool 15 to 20 minutes. Cut in squares and serve.

Makes 6 servings.

CUSTARD SAUCE

¼ cup butter or margarine
3 cups milk
⅓ cup flour (instant-type preferred)

½ teaspoon salt
4 eggs

Melt butter in a large saucepan. Add 2 cups of the milk. Heat slowly. Mix remaining 1 cup milk, flour, and salt in a small bowl. Add to milk and butter mixture. Stir until mixture begins to thicken; remove from heat.

Beat eggs in a small bowl. Spoon several tablespoons of thickened sauce into eggs. (This will temper the eggs and prevent curdling.) Add to custard; mix well. Cook about 2 minutes longer.

PIE CRUST MIX

6 cups unsifted all-purpose
    flour
2 teaspoons salt

2 cups cold shortening
Cold water

Mix flour and salt in a large bowl.

Using a pastry cutter, cut in shortening until mixture resembles small peas. (Do not overmix—blend only until shortening forms small particles with the flour.) Use a rubber spatula to scrape sides of bowl.

For single-crust pie: Mix 1½ cups pie crust mixture with 2 to 3 tablespoons cold water. Let rest 10 minutes. Roll out.

For double-crust pie: Mix 3 cups pie crust mixture with 4 to 5 tablespoons cold water. Let rest 10 minutes. Roll out.

Pie crust mixture can be stored in jars or shortening cans on cupboard shelves. DO NOT ADD WATER when storing.

The following chart illustrates how much pie crust mix to use depending on pie pan size and number of crusts.

Pie Pan Size	Single Crust	Double Crust
8 inch	1 to 1½ cups	2 to 2¼ cups
9 inch	1½ cups	2½ cups
10 inch	1¾ cups	2¾ cups
12 tart shells	2¾ cups	

PIZZA AND PIZZA TOPPING

Store-bought pizzas will be less appealing to you after you have tried this topping on homemade Mediterranean dough made into pizza or on English Muffins, or even on commercial French bread.

Dough for 1 loaf
   Mediterranean Bread
   (see Index for recipe)
2 cups tomatoes and tomato
   sauce mixture (can be
   purchased mixed in 15-
   ounce cans)
2 teaspoons Italian herb
   (available in the spice
   rack in supermarkets)
1 clove garlic, finely
   minced or pressed
2 tablespoons grated
   Parmesan or Romano
   cheese or a combination
   of both

2 tablespoons olive or
   vegetable oil
2 tablespoons fresh parsley,
   finely minced
1 pound cooked, spicy
   sausage of your choice,
   crumbled (Italian
   preferred)
4 tablespoons vegetable oil
2 cups grated mozzarella,
   Swiss, or Monterey
   Jack cheese

Make crust for pizza by preparing dough for 1 loaf of Mediterranean Bread. Divide dough in half.

Mix remaining ingredients except 4 tablespoons oil and 2 cups cheese, in a large bowl.

Spread 2 tablespoons oil on two 12-inch round pizza pans or a baking sheet. Stretch dough as far as possible in pan. Let dough rest 10 to 20 minutes; then continue stretching to edge of pans.

Heat oven to 475°. Cover each pizza with tomato mixture. Bake pizza 20 to 25 minutes. Spread cheese over top of pizzas; bake 5 minutes longer. Serve immediately.

Makes 2 pizzas.

POLENTA

Try this popular northern Italian meal as a delicious change from pasta.

3 cups water   1 cup cold water
1 cup yellow cornmeal   1 teaspoon salt

Heat 3 cups water to boiling in a heavy-duty pan. Mix cornmeal, cold water, and salt. Add cornmeal mixture slowly to boiling water, beating with a wire whisk. Stir with wooden spoon for 2 minutes. Reduce heat to very low. Cover; cook about 10 minutes. (Be very careful when stirring or removing lid that cornmeal mixture does not bubble up and burn you.)

Pour cornmeal mixture into greased loaf pan. Cover directly with plastic wrap. Cool; refrigerate.

To serve, slice Polenta. Heat covered. Place on serving dish. Top with spaghetti sauce or Ratatouille (see Index) and serve with Italian sausage of your choice.

Makes 6 servings.

PORK PASTIES

Introduced by Welsh miners, delicious pasties are found in roadside stands and at church suppers in northern Michigan.

Pie crust sufficient for 6
   pasties (about 4 cups)
   (See Index for Pie
   Crust recipe)
½ pound cooked sausage
   meat

1 to 2 turnips and/or 1 to 2
   carrots, pared
1 to 2 potatoes, pared
1 medium onion, thinly
   sliced
Salt and pepper to taste
1 egg white, beaten

Sauté sausage in a lightly oiled frying pan. Drain and cool. Reserve. Mince all vegetables; combine. Sprinkle with salt and pepper.

Roll out dough to ⅛-inch thickness. Cut out to 6-inch circles.

Heat oven to 425°.

Divide the vegetables among dough circles, covering half of each circle to within ¼ inch of the edge. Divide the sausage into 6 parts; arrange sausage on top of the vegetables. Brush the edges of each circle with egg white. Fold the pastry over the filling, forming half circles. Seal by pressing with the tines of a fork. Pierce tops.

Bake pasties on baking sheet for 10 minutes. Reduce heat to 375°. Bake for about 15 minutes longer (baking time will depend on the size of the meat and vegetables).

Makes 6 pasties.

RATATOUILLE NIÇOISE

This dish has its origin in southern France and has gained great popularity among all people who enjoy special foods.

⅓ cup vegetable oil
1 to 2 cloves garlic, crushed
¾ cup thinly sliced onion
2 to 3 green peppers, seeded, cut into julienne strips
2½ cups diced eggplant (pared, if desired)
3 cups zucchini, cut into 1-inch slices and then cut in half

1 28-ounce can Italian plum tomatoes or 1 15-ounce can tomato sauce
1 to 2 teaspoons Italian herb (available in the spice rack in supermarkets)
Salt and pepper to taste
12 Italian olives, pitted, cut in half

Heat oil in heavy large saucepan or Dutch oven. Add garlic; cook until golden, not brown. Remove garlic. Add onions; saute until soft but not brown. Add green peppers, eggplant, and zucchini; cook until light brown, stirring frequently without crushing vegetables. Add tomatoes and seasonings.

If ratatouille is to be served immediately, heat mixture to boiling. Reduce heat; simmer until vegetables are soft but not mushy.

If ratatouille is to be served at a later time, heat mixture to boiling. Remove from heat. Cool; refrigerate. At serving time, heat oven to 400°. Place mixture in casserole dish. Bake uncovered for 30 minutes, stirring once or twice during that period. (If ratatouille is reducing too fast, cover casserole dish.)

Serve ratatouille accompanied by or combined with cooked Italian sausage of your choice. (1½ pounds will serve 6 people.)

Ratatouille can also be served cold as an appetizer or part of an antipasto garnished with the olives. Serve with French bread.

Note: In summer 2 cups chopped, seeded, peeled fresh tomatoes can be substituted for the canned tomatoes.

REFRIED BEANS

Nutritious beans served Mexican-style will provide variety for your meals.

1 pound pinto beans   **⅓ to ½ cup water**
1 teaspoon salt   **1 clove garlic, minced or**
⅓ cup vegetable oil   **pressed**

Soak beans by the quick method: Place beans in a large saucepan or Dutch oven. Wash beans and discard any discolored ones or any foreign matter. Generously cover beans with water. Heat beans to boiling; remove from heat. Cover; let stand 1 hour. Drain water (this step is very important to avoid the distressing elements of beans). Again cover beans with cold water; add salt and cook beans until tender. (Taste beans to determine tenderness.)

Mix 2 cups cooked beans, oil, water, and garlic in a large frying pan. Mash beans to a pulp with a masher. Sauté bean mixture slowly to enhance flavor, stirring frequently and adding more water if necessary.

Use in any recipe calling for refried beans. Any leftover boiled beans can be frozen or used for a bean soup.

Makes 2 cups.

SAUSAGE AND SALAD VEGETABLES

Have you ever wondered what to do with the leaf trimmings from your salad greens—iceberg lettuce, romaine, endive, escarole, cabbage, etc.? Taste this!

4 to 5 cups salad trimmings
1 pound sausage meat of
    your choice (without
    casings)
2 cloves garlic, finely
    minced

Wash all salad trimmings thoroughly. Trim outside leaves and tips of heads. Chop trimmings coarsely.

Sauté sausage in a lightly oiled frying pan until light brown. Stir and crumble sausage while sautéing. Drain all but 3 tablespoons fat from pan. Remove sausage; reserve.

Boil trimmings in a small amount of water until wilted. Drain and squeeze out water.

Add garlic to frying pan with sausage drippings; add vegetables and sausage. Stir until combined and thoroughly heated.

Makes 6 servings.

SAUSAGE BURRITOS

For busy days, this is a good make-ahead dish to be heated at serving time. Burritos make wonderful eating for lunch, dinner, or late evening.

1 cup Refried Beans (see Index for recipe)
1 pound mildly seasoned loose sausage meat of your choice
¼ cup minced onion
1 green chili pepper, chopped
2 cloves garlic, finely minced or pressed
1 cup tomato sauce
1 teaspoon cumin
1 teaspoon chili powder
½ teaspoon ground coriander
Salt and pepper to taste
¼ cup vegetable oil
6 large flour tortillas
1 cup dairy sour cream
6 to 8 ounces shredded Muenster or Monterey Jack cheese
Dairy sour cream or guacamole
Chopped green onions
Finely diced fresh tomatoes

Prepare Refried Beans.

Sauté sausage, onion, and chili pepper in a lightly oiled frying pan until soft but not brown. Add garlic; sauté until garlic is golden. Add refried beans and tomato sauce. Add spices; stir well. Simmer mixture 10 minutes to blend flavors. Taste and adjust seasonings, if desired.

Heat oven to 350°. Heat tortillas one at a time to soften, about 10 seconds in a frying pan with oil. Turn tortilla to soften second side, about 10 seconds. To assemble, spread each tortilla with 2 tablespoons sour cream and sausage mixture, evenly divided among tortillas. Roll tortilla part way, tuck in edges, and continue to roll up. Place burritos in a lightly oiled baking pan, seam sides down. Sprinkle 2 to 3 tablespoons cheese on top of each burrito.

Bake until burritos are warm and cheese is melted, about 15 minutes.

Serve burritos with additional sour cream or guacamole, chopped green onions, and finely diced tomatoes.

Makes 6 burritos.

SAUSAGE CORN MUFFINS

This recipe can become a complete breakfast when served with fruit and beverage and is hearty enough for luncheon, served with soup or salad.

1 8-ounce can whole kernel corn, drained (reserve liquid)
1 egg
⅓ cup instant nonfat dry milk
2 tablespoons vegetable oil

¼ cup sugar
1¼ cups cornmeal
1 cup all-purpose flour
4 teaspoons baking powder
½ teaspoon salt
½ pound sausage meat, cooked

Heat oven to 400°.

Drain can of corn, reserving liquid and corn. Mix corn liquid with water to make 1 cup. Beat egg in a large bowl; add corn liquid, dry milk, oil, and sugar. Mix well.

Mix cornmeal, flour, baking powder, and salt. Add all at once to liquid mixture. Stir only; do not beat. Add reserved corn and sausage; stir again. Bake in a greased baking dish, 9 inches square, 20 to 25 minutes. Batter can also be poured into a well-greased, 12-cup muffin pan and baked for 15 to 20 minutes. (Use a spring-type ice cream scoop to pour batter in muffin cups.)

Remove from oven. Place on rack. Cool 5 minutes and serve.

Makes 10 squares or 12 muffins.

SAUSAGE DRESSING

Here is a tasty dressing—ideal for chicken, turkey, or pork—which is hearty enough to extend the meat dish you are serving.

½ pound loose sausage meat
1 cup chopped onions
1 cup peeled, finely sliced
   celery
3 cups firm-textured fresh
   bread cubes

1 tablespoon poultry
   seasoning
½ teaspoon salt
¼ cup finely minced fresh
   parsley

Sauté loose sausage gently in a lightly oiled frying pan over high heat for 2 or 3 minutes. Reduce heat; add onions and celery. Cook until vegetables are soft but not brown. Reserve.

Mix bread cubes, poultry seasoning, salt, and parsley in a large bowl. Toss together gently. Add sausage mixture; stir.

Dressing can be made 1 day in advance and refrigerated. Do not stuff turkey or chicken with dressing until just before roasting.

This dressing is sufficient for a 10- to 12-pound turkey or 2 chickens.

SAUSAGE HASH

The savory quality of this dish will surprise you. Don't delay trying it.

2 to 3 potatoes, pared
1 green pepper
2 medium onions

1 pound loose sausage meat
   of your choice
2 to 3 tablespoons water
Salt to taste

Coarsely grind or finely dice potatoes, pepper, and onions.

Sauté sausage in a frying pan until some of the fat has exuded. Drain. Add potatoes and water; stir. Cover and cook 5 minutes. Add pepper and onions. Gently cook uncovered, stirring frequently, until potatoes and sausage are cooked and onions and pepper are soft. Taste and add salt, if desired.

Serve immediately, with a poached egg placed over hash, if desired.

Note: To poach eggs: Allow 1 or 2 eggs per person. Boil water in a large frying pan. Add ½ teaspoon distilled white vinegar. Reduce heat; crack eggs and carefully slip into gently simmering water. Cover and cook until eggs reach desired doneness. Remove with slotted spoon and place on hash.

Makes 4 to 6 servings.

SAUSAGE IN ORANGE-RAISIN SAUCE

This unusual dish is flavorful and nutritious.

1½ pounds mild flavored
    sausage links
3 tablespoons cornstarch
2 cups orange juice
2 tablespoons sugar
1 tablespoon finely minced
    onion
½ teaspoon dry mustard

¼ teaspoon ground ginger
1 teaspoon distilled white
    vinegar
½ cup raisins
2 oranges, sectioned, or 1
    small can mandarin
    oranges

Sauté sausage in a lightly oiled frying pan until brown and almost completely cooked; reserve.

Mix cornstarch and ½ cup of the orange juice in a large saucepan. Add remaining juice (if using mandarin oranges, drained juice may be included in the orange juice), sugar, onion, mustard, ginger and vinegar. Stir well and add raisins. Heat mixture, stirring constantly, until it thickens and comes to a boil. Add orange sections and reserved sausages; heat. Serve immediately or can be reheated for later use. Serve with steamed rice.

Makes 6 servings.

SAUSAGE KEBABS

These can be served in miniature for cocktail parties or in larger sizes for meals. Everyone loves the ease and fun of skewers.

1½ pounds sausage meat of
    your choice
1 egg white, beaten
2 green peppers, cut into
    1-inch squares
20 pineapple chunks,
    drained

20 sweet pickled onions,
    drained
2 tablespoons vegetable oil
12 thin skewers, 6 inches
    long

Mix sausage and egg white well. Form into 1-inch balls. Sauté balls in a lightly oiled frying pan until brown. Blanch green peppers in boiling water 2 minutes. Drain. Immediately plunge peppers into cold water and drain again.

Mix peppers, pineapple, and onions in a large bowl. Toss with vegetable oil to coat. Skewer ingredients as follows: Pepper, sausage ball, pineapple, sausage ball, and onion. Repeat. Refrigerate kebabs until serving time.

To serve, place skewers under preheated broiler or 400° oven until hot. Serve immediately. For dinner, serve kebabs with steamed rice.

Makes 4 to 6 servings.

SAUSAGE LOAF IN CRUST

To give your sausage a fancy dimension, encase it in crust. It's a delicious idea for family or parties. The flavor of the dish will vary with type of sausage you choose.

2 pounds sausage meat of
    your choice
2 egg whites, lightly beaten
¼ cup finely minced fresh
    parsley

Prepared pie crust for a
    double-crust pie (see
    Index for Pie Crust Mix
    recipe)

Prepare pie crust, but do not roll out.

Mix sausage meat, egg whites, and parsley thoroughly in a large bowl. Shape mixture into a roll about 3 inches in diameter. Place roll on a broiler pan which has a rack for draining fat. Bake at 350° 40 to 45 minutes. Remove from oven; cool completely.

Roll out pie crust. Place sausage roll in center of pie crust; enclose the sausage roll with pie crust. Refrigerate lightly covered with wax paper.

Thirty minutes before serving time, heat oven to 425°. Bake sausage loaf until crust is brown and sausage is heated, 15 to 20 minutes. Slice and serve. Loaf is delicious with au gratin potatoes and cooked-just-right broccoli.

Makes 6 servings.

SAUSAGE 'N' SAUERKRAUT BALLS

When these hors d'oeuvres are served even those who don't like sauerkraut will find them irresistible!

1 pound sausage meat
   (breakfast type)
1 medium onion, finely
   minced
1 tablespoon finely chopped
   fresh parsley
½ clove garlic, finely
   minced or pressed
½ cup water
⅓ cup flour (instant
   preferred)

1 pound (3 cups)
   sauerkraut ground,
   well drained
2 eggs
¼ cup water
½ cup flour (instant
   preferred)
2 cups dry bread crumbs
Deep fat for frying

Sauté sausage lightly in a lightly oiled frying pan; add onion and cook until onion is soft but not brown. Drain excessive fat. Add parsley and garlic; mix well. Remove from heat.

Blend ½ cup water and ⅓ cup flour until smooth. Stir into sausage mixture. Add sauerkraut; mix well. Return mixture to heat. Cook over low heat 2 to 3 minutes. Remove from heat. Cool; refrigerate until completely cold.

Shape mixture into small balls about the size of a walnut. Beat eggs with ¼ cup water. Roll balls in ½ cup flour, egg mixture, and then bread crumbs. Refrigerate breaded balls at least 30 minutes.

Fry breaded balls in deep fat (375°) until brown, 1 to 2 minutes. Serve immediately with horseradish mayonnaise sauce.

Makes about 50 balls.

SAUSAGE PUFFS

These are quick appetizers. To make sure they are served hot, bake them after your guests arrive.

1 package round,
    butterflake,
    refrigerated rolls
1 cup cooked, crumbled,
    mild-flavored sausage

2 to 3 tablespoons
    mayonnaise
4 tablespoons grated
    Parmesan or Romano
    cheese

Heat oven to 400°.

Split each roll in half and flatten to stretch. Mix remaining ingredients in a small bowl. Place 1 teaspoon of mixture in the center of each split roll. Pinch together to close tightly, place puffs pinched side down on greased baking sheet.

Bake puffs for 5 to 6 minutes or until lightly browned. Serve immediately.

Makes 16 puffs.

SAUSAGE SALAD

Popular in Europe, this salad is made of any combination of vegetables. Select your vegetables for color and flavor and try this recipe soon for luncheons and buffets.

French Dressing (recipe
   follows)
1 pound spicy sausage
   (Sunday Breakfast
   Sausage is a good
   choice)

4 ribs celery
1 sweet onion, Bermuda or
   Spanish

Make French Dressing.

Simmer sausage gently in water to cover until thoroughly cooked. Cool. Slice sausage diagonally into 1¼-inch pieces. Peel celery; cut diagonally into ¼-inch pieces.

SALAD INGREDIENTS OF YOUR CHOICE

Assemble salad ingredients. All blanched or cooked vegetables must be drained, quickly rinsed in cold water, and drained again. This will retain the color and stop the cooking process.

(About 1 to 2 cups of any 3
   or 4 selections)
Carrots, thick sliced and
   crisply cooked
Cauliflower, broken into
   flowerettes and
   blanched
Cucumber, pared, cut into
   ½-inch slices, halved,
   seeds removed
Garbanzo (ceci) or dry
   white beans, cooked
Green beans, crisply
   cooked, drained

Green pepper, slivered and
   raw or slivered and
   blanched
Potatoes, sliced, cooked
   until tender
Small shell macaroni,
   cooked but not soft
Ripe olives, pitted or
   pimiento-stuffed green
   olives
Tomato wedges
Hard-cooked eggs

FRENCH DRESSING

1 cup vegetable oil
⅓ cup red or white wine
   vinegar
½ teaspoon dry mustard
½ teaspoon salt
½ teaspoon freshly ground
   black pepper

Chopped fresh herbs or
  ½ teaspoon dry Italian
  herb
Salt (optional)

Mix all ingredients together and shake thoroughly to form an emulsion. Using an ice cube will help thicken the dressing.

Combine sausage, celery, onion, and selected vegetable in a large bowl. Mix salad with dressing, ¼ to ½ cup depending on the amount of salad prepared. Refrigerate at least 1 hour. Taste and adjust dressing and salt, if desired.

Serve salad garnished with tomato wedges and hard-cooked eggs.

Makes at least 6 servings.

SAUSAGE SAUTÉ

This simple, hot sandwich is very appealing for lunch, dinner, or a late evening meal. Partially cooked sausage can be refrigerated and the vegetables added later for a quick meal.

1 large green pepper
2 large onions

1 pound sausage,
   preferably Italian,
   Polish, or a well-
   seasoned sausage

Remove top, seeds, and membrane from green pepper. Slice lengthwise in narrow slivers. Peel and slice onions.

Sauté sausage gently in a lightly oiled frying pan until about half cooked. Add pepper and onions. Cook until sausage is brown and thoroughly cooked.

Serve sausage and vegetables on a crusty roll or French bread.

Makes 4 servings.

SAUSAGE-SAUERKRAUT FILLED BREAD

Here is an unusual bread that can be used as an hors d'oeuvre, or for luncheon or a snack. It's delicious with potato salad.

Dough for 1 loaf
   Mediterranean Bread
   (see Index for recipe)
½ pound loose sausage meat
   of your choice
   (Breakfast Sausage),
   Milwaukee Sausage, or
   Italian Sausage—No
   Seed are good
   selections)

1 cup sauerkraut,
   thoroughly drained
½ cup chopped onion
1 tablespoon instant flour

Prepare dough for 1 loaf Mediterranean Bread.

Sauté sausage in a lightly oiled frying pan until lightly brown but not completely cooked. Drain all but 2 tablespoons fat from pan.

Taste sauerkraut. If salty, wash before using. Squeeze out all water. Sauté sauerkraut and onion in reserved sausage drippings until soft but not brown. Remove from heat; add sausage and stir well. Cool.

Roll dough out on floured board to about ½-inch thickness. Spread cooled filling on dough; roll tightly in a jelly-roll fashion. Place in a greased loaf pan, 8½ × 5 × 3 inches. Cover and let rise in a warm spot until dough almost reaches top of pan. Heat oven to 400°.

Cover dough with greased aluminum foil. Place a baking sheet on foil and a weight on top of baking sheet. This will keep the bread from unrolling during baking.

Bake bread for 30 minutes. Uncover and bake 10 minutes longer to brown top. Remove from oven and baking pan; cool on rack. Cool completely before serving.

Makes 1 loaf.

SAUSAGE SPAGHETTI SAUCE

Here is your opportunity to use the pork bones you saved from your sausage making. This recipe makes a savory and meat-flavored sauce that you will appreciate.

Pork or beef bones of any
quantity
1 to 1½ pounds sausage
meat or sausage in
casings (Italian or well-
seasoned type)
1 onion, diced
1 clove garlic, minced or
pressed
1 28-ounce can Italian-style
plum tomatoes

8 ounces tomato sauce or
paste
4 sprigs fresh parsley,
chopped
1 to 2 teaspoons Italian
herb (available in the
spice rack in
supermarkets)
¼ cup vermouth (optional)
Salt to taste

Brown bones under broiler. Brown sausage in a large saucepan or Dutch oven; reserve.

Sauté onion and garlic lightly in the saucepan. Add bones, tomatoes, tomato sauce, parsley, Italian herb, and vermouth. Simmer gently for 1 hour. Remove bones; add sausage. Simmer for 30 minutes. Taste for salt. Serve sauce over spaghetti.

Makes 4 cups.

SAUSAGE-SQUASH BAKE

A good friend, Charlotte Budde of Detroit, contributed this marvelous recipe. A meal complete with vegetables, the dish is ideal for a buffet, potluck supper, or a make-ahead family dinner.

1 pound sausage of your choice (mildly seasoned preferred)
½ cup chopped onion
½ cup slivered green peppers
1 cup fresh mushrooms, or drained, canned mushrooms

2 medium yellow summer squash, unpared
¼ cup instant flour
2 cups rich chicken stock
3 ounces cream cheese, cut into small pieces
Salt and white pepper to taste
1 cup cooked rice

Crumble and sauté sausage in a lightly oiled frying pan until lightly browned. Drain all but 1 tablespoon fat; reserve sausage. Sauté onion, peppers, and mushrooms, if fresh, in fat in frying pan. Reserve. Slice squash; boil in water to barely cover for 2 minutes. Drain. Add flour to cold chicken stock; cook in saucepan over medium heat until thickened. Add cream cheese; stir until cheese has melted. Add salt and pepper to sauce. Heat oven to 350°. Combine cooked vegetables and rice in a greased, 2-quart casserole dish. Add sauce; mix gently. Top with sausage; bake covered for 20 to 25 minutes. Uncover; bake 10 minutes longer. Allow to rest 10 minutes before serving.

Makes 6 servings.

SAUSAGE-ZUCCHINI QUICHE

This hearty quiche is substantial enough for dinner. Served with a crisp green salad, it makes a nutritionally sound meal.

10-inch pie shell (see Index
    for Pie Crust Mix
    recipe)
3 eggs
1½ cups milk or a mixture
    of milk and half-and-
    half
2 tablespoons flour (instant
    type preferred)
½ teaspoon salt

⅛ teaspoon ground nutmeg
1 small zucchini
¼ teaspoon salt
½ pound mildly seasoned
    sausage meat
1 medium-size onion, finely
    diced
4 ounces Swiss or Gruyère
    cheese, grated

Make pie shell. Bake at 425° for no longer than 10 minutes. Remove from oven; cool.

Beat eggs in a large bowl. Add milk, flour, ½ teaspoon salt, and nutmeg. Mix thoroughly. Reserve.

Grate zucchini; sprinkle with ¼ teaspoon salt. Let rest 10 minutes.

Sauté sausage meat in a lightly oiled frying pan until light brown. Drain excess fat. Add onion; continue to cook. Drain zucchini; rinse and squeeze out all water. Add to sausage and onion. Cook 1 minute, stirring occasionally. Heat oven to 375°. Spoon sausage mixture into the cooled pie shell. Pour in reserved egg mixture. Sprinkle grated cheese over top. Bake for about 45 minutes. (Center should still be slightly soft when removed from oven.) Cool 10 minutes. Cut into serving size pieces for 6.

Makes 6 servings.

SCOTTISH EGGS

What is a better combination than eggs and sausage? This is a favorite of the people of Scotland and it will become yours, too.

6 hard-cooked eggs, cooled
1 pound pork sausage meat
1 egg white, beaten
½ cup instant flour

1 egg, beaten
1 cup dry bread crumbs
Vegetable oil for deep fat
    frying

Peel eggs and dry. Mix sausage meat and the beaten egg white thoroughly. Coat eggs with flour. Wrap sausage meat around each egg. Coat again with flour. Dip eggs in beaten egg, then bread crumbs. Refrigerate at least 30 minutes or until coating dries.

Heat oil to 375°, deep enough to cover eggs. Fry eggs until lightly browned. Drain on paper toweling. Eggs can be served hot or cold as hors d'oeuvres or for any meal.

Makes 6 servings.

SPÄTZLE

These always popular "soft noodles" are fast and easy to make, and good for many meals. Try this simple method using a basket.

2 eggs
½ cup water
1¾ cups all-purpose flour
½ teaspoon salt

¼ teaspoon baking powder
Water
¼ cup butter

Beat eggs and water. Add remaining ingredients except butter. Mix until well blended. Consistency should be of a heavy batter.

Heat water in saucepan until rapidly boiling. Pour batter through very large hole colander-like basket (many deep fryers come with baskets suitable for making spätzle) into water. Simmer 4 or 5 minutes. Cover; let stand 2 to 3 minutes. Drain thoroughly. Add butter; stir well.

Spätzle can be reheated. Heat prepared spätzle in pan with 2 to 4 additional tablespoons butter or margarine. For a crunchy addition, add ¼ cup corn flakes to the butter while heating.

Serve spätzle immediately with sausage of your choice.

Makes 4 to 6 servings.

STUFFED BREAD

Served warm, this will make an excellent appetizer or snack that no one can resist.

Dough for 1 loaf
   Mediterranean Bread
   (see Index for recipe)

**1 pound sausage of your
choice, in casings**

Prepare the dough.

While dough is rising, simmer sausage gently in water to cover. Drain water; dry sausage. Sauté in a lightly oiled frying pan until light brown. Cool; reserve sausage.

After the dough has risen once, shape into a ball. Let rest 10 minutes covered.

Roll dough out with rolling pin to about 1 inch thickness. Place sausage on dough; roll dough into a long cylinder around the length of sausage. Place on greased baking sheet seam side down; let rise until doubled in size.

Heat oven to 400°. Bake loaf about 40 minutes. Cool. To serve, cut loaf into slices.

Makes 1 loaf.

STUFFED PEPPERS ITALIANO

If you follow this recipe, there will be no complaints about the indigestible juices of green peppers. These peppers are tasty, and different from the hamburger-stuffed variety.

3 large green peppers
1½ quarts water
1½ pounds mild Italian
   Sausage—No Fennel or
   a sausage of your
   choice
¼ cup diced onion

½ cup partially cooked rice
1 cup tomato sauce
2 tablespoons finely
   chopped fresh parsley
2 tablespoons freshly
   grated Parmesan or
   Romano cheese

Wash peppers; remove tops. Cut peppers in half; remove seeds and membrane. Heat water to boiling in a large saucepan or Dutch oven; blanch peppers 2 minutes. Remove peppers from water; immediately pour cold water over peppers to stop cooking action and retain color. Drain and reserve. Sauté sausage and onion in a frying pan until light brown. Drain fat. Mix sausage, rice, half the tomato sauce, parsley, and cheese in a large bowl. Stir well. Stuff peppers generously with sausage mixture.

Heat oven to 350°. Bake peppers in a shallow, greased pan about 50 minutes. Ten minutes before peppers are done, place a spoonful of remaining tomato sauce on each pepper. Serve peppers immediately. Leftover peppers can be frozen.

Makes 6 servings.

STUFFED SHELLS

These shells are very large and six will provide an adequate meal for one person. For convenience, you can make them in advance, then refrigerate.

3 quarts water
1 teaspoon salt
36 No. 67 macaroni shells
   (about 1 pound)
1 package (10 ounces)
   frozen, chopped
   spinach
1 pound loose sausage meat,
   Italian or a sausage of
   your choice
¼ cup finely minced onion
½ cup diced fresh
   mushrooms

1 clove garlic, finely
   minced or pressed
½ teaspoon Italian herb
   (available in the spice
   rack in supermarkets)
½ teaspoon salt
¼ teaspoon ground nutmeg
¼ cup freshly grated
   Parmesan or Romano
   cheese
¼ cup dry bread crumbs
Spaghetti sauce
Grated Parmesan or
   Romano cheese

Heat 3 quarts water and 1 teaspoon salt to boiling. Cook shells in boiling water until tender but still underdone. Drain and reserve.

Cook spinach according to package instructions. Drain; squeeze out excess water.

Sauté sausage in a lightly oiled frying pan. Add onion; cook until onion is soft but not brown. Drain some of the fat from pan. Add mushrooms and garlic; sauté 1 minute. Remove from heat. Add spinach, Italian herb, ½ teaspoon salt, and the nutmeg. Stir gently. Add cheese and bread crumbs; stir again.

Heat oven to 375°. Stuff shells generously with sausage mixture. Place shells loosely in a lightly oiled baking dish. Cover with spaghetti sauce. Bake until hot, about 20 minutes.

Serve with additional grated cheese.

Makes 6 servings.

STUFFED ZUCCHINI

Here is a tasty dish for lunch. Serve it for dinner with elbow macaroni tossed with butter and freshly grated Parmesan cheese.

4 medium zucchini
½ pound loose sausage meat
¼ cup finely chopped onion
1 clove garlic, minced or
    pressed
1 medium-size fresh tomato,
    peeled, chopped, or 2
    canned tomatoes,
    drained

½ teaspoon salt
1 cup grated fresh bread
    crumbs made from
    firm-textured bread
½ cup tomato sauce

Wash zucchini; trim ends. Cut zucchini in half lengthwise. With a spoon, scoop out center pulp; reserve pulp. Simmer zucchini shells in boiling water 1 minute. Drain and reserve.

Sauté sausage gently in a lightly oiled frying pan. Add onion and reserved zucchini pulp. Cook until vegetables are soft but not brown. Add garlic, tomato, and salt; sauté 1 or 2 minutes longer. Remove from heat; drain excess fat.

Heat oven to 350°. Mix bread crumbs and sausage mixture in a large bowl; mix well. Stuff zucchini generously with sausage mixture. Place in a shallow, greased pan and bake about 30 minutes. Spread tops of zucchinis with tomato sauce; bake 15 minutes longer.

Serve hot.

Makes 4 servings.

SWEET-SOUR FRUITED SAUSAGE

This combination is so satisfying you won't need any dessert. Serve it with a salad to make a complete meal.

1½ pounds mild-flavored sausage in casings
1 can (1 pound, 4 ounces) pineapple chunks (pear halves may be substituted)
¼ cup sugar
3 tablespoons cornstarch
1 teaspoon ground ginger or 1 tablespoon fresh ginger root, finely minced

½ cup water
⅓ cup distilled white vinegar
1 tablespoon soy sauce
1 cup seedless green grapes, canned or fresh
12 maraschino cherries, cut in half
Steamed rice

Sauté sausage slowly in a lightly oiled frying pan until brown and thoroughly cooked. Drain fat; reserve sausage.

Drain pineapple, reserving juice. Mix sugar, cornstarch, and ginger in a large saucepan. Add reserved pineapple juice, water, vinegar, and soy sauce. Mix well. Cook, stirring constantly, until mixture thickens and becomes clear. Add sausage, pineapple chunks, grapes, and cherries. Stir carefully until heated thoroughly. Serve over steamed rice.

Makes 6 servings.

SWEET-SOUR RED CABBAGE

You will enjoy this dish on your menu, accompanied by a tasty sausage. The hint of orange imparts an interesting change.

1 medium-size head red cabbage (about 2 pounds)
1 medium-size onion, minced
¼ cup vegetable oil
2 apples (hard varieties such as Jonathan or Golden Delicious), pared, chopped
1 teaspoon salt

½ cup dry red wine or ¼ cup distilled white vinegar
1 tablespoon dry orange powder mix (such as used for breakfast drinks)
2 tablespoons sugar
2 teaspoons cornstarch
3 tablespoons water

Shred cabbage, discarding the core and outer leaves. Rinse in cold water. Drain shredded cabbage, allowing water to cling to pieces.

Sauté onion in oil in a frying pan until soft but not brown. Add cabbage to onion. Cover and let simmer until cabbage is wilted. Add apples, salt, and wine. Cook about 45 minutes, adding water if necessary.

Mix orange powder, sugar, cornstarch, and 3 tablespoons water. Add to cabbage; stir and cook about 5 minutes.

Serve with sausage of your choice which has no predominant taste.

Makes 6 servings.

TACOS

This is a special treat made with chili sausage. Be sure to make plenty for teenagers.

1½ pounds chili sausage
¼ cup vegetable oil
12 corn tortillas
2 cups refried beans
3 tomatoes, diced
1 large sweet onion,
    thinly sliced, separated
    into rings

2 cups shredded lettuce
1 cup shredded Monterey
    Jack or colby cheese
Dairy sour cream (optional)
Salsa sauce (optional)

Crumble sausage and sauté in a lightly oiled frying pan until thoroughly cooked. Reserve and keep warm.

Heat vegetable oil in a large frying pan. Quickly cook tortilla in oil on each side to soften. Fold in half and hold with tongs until golden brown. Place tortillas in a paper towel-lined bowl; keep warm. Continue process until all tortillas have been cooked.

To serve, place cooked sausage and refried beans in separate bowls. Arrange tomatoes, onion, lettuce, and cheese on a platter. Wrap tortillas in a napkin to keep warm.

To fill taco shells, spread beans and sausage; then layer cheese, tomatoes, onions, and lettuce.

Serve with sour cream or salsa sauce, if desired.

Makes 6 servings.

TZATZÍKI SAUCE

Serve this tangy sauce as a dip with fresh vegetables, or use in other recipes as indicated.

2 cucumbers, pared, seeds removed, grated, drained
1 to 2 cloves garlic, finely minced or pressed
½ teaspoon salt
¼ teaspoon ground white pepper
1 teaspoon distilled white vinegar
¼ cup vegetable oil
1 pound plain thick yogurt

Mix all ingredients except yogurt. Add yogurt; beat mixture on medium speed in mixer bowl until mixture has a creamy appearance. Prepare sauce a day in advance to blend flavors.

Makes about 3 cups.

YORKSHIRE PUDDING OR POPOVER SAUSAGE

In a baking dish, it is called Yorkshire pudding; in individual muffin cups they are called popovers. Either way, don't miss this easily prepared treat.

1 pound mildly seasoned sausage
2 eggs
1 cup milk
1 cup all-purpose flour
½ teaspoon salt

Crumble sausage; place in a baking dish 8 × 12 inches, or divide sausage among 8 to 10 muffin cups. Heat oven to 450°. Heat sausage in oven about 10 minutes.

While sausage is heating, beat eggs and milk in a medium-sized bowl. Mix flour and salt; add to egg mixture. Mix well.

Remove baking dish or muffin tin from oven; immediately pour egg mixture over sausage (this is a thin batter). Return to oven; bake 20 to 25 minutes. Serve immediately.

Makes 6 to 8 servings.

Chapter 11

We who live in a major metropolitan area are blessed with an abundance of suppliers for almost any product.

If you have difficulty obtaining sausage making supplies, we will try to locate them for you. Just drop a note to:

Bernadine Sellers Rechner
P. O. Box 75
Prospect Heights, IL 60070

Chapter 12

METRIC MEASURES

Weights

1 ounce equals 30 grams
1 pound equals 454 grams
1 pound equals .454 kilograms
1 kilogram equals 2.2 pounds

Volumes

1 quart equals .96 liters
1 liter equals 1.05 quarts
1 gallon equals 3.83 liters

HANDY EQUIVALENTS

3 teaspoons equal 1 tablespoon
2 tablespoons equal 1 fluid ounce
4 tablespoons equal ¼ cup
5 tablespoons plus 1 teaspoon equal ⅓ cup
8 tablespoons equal ½ cup
10 tablespoons plus 2 teaspoons equal ⅔ cup
12 tablespoons equal ¾ cup
16 tablespoons equal 1 cup
1 cup equals ½ pint
2 cups equal 1 pint
4 cups equal 1 quart
4 quarts equal 1 gallon
8 quarts equal 1 peck
4 pecks equal 1 bushel

Acknowledgments

I am grateful to all my family. My mother, who never used a recipe, taught me to be creative. My father took me to wholesale meat suppliers where he selected meat for our family retail store when I was only five or six years old. My four sisters and two brothers have also contributed to the development of my culinary abilities.

Without Bruno Elmer, one of my many instructors at the Culinary Institute of America, I would not have developed the critical tasting abilities so necessary to create these recipes.

Al Wilkin's vast knowledge of the meat industry and his interest in this book provided me with support and background knowledge. Joe Matusiewicz assisted me greatly by answering my questions about sausage and spices. Joe LoDolce has helped me purchase the exact cuts and quality of meat I've wanted.

Alex Kruzel, administrator of the MONNACEP program where I have taught for 15 years, permitted me to develop new food courses and programs. Elaine Sherman, co-owner of the Complete Cook in Deerfield, Illinois, did the same. Elaine offered me many opportunities at her cooking school and cookware store. My students' curiosity demanded my continued education and has brought new experiences to my life. Becky Dieterloff carefully typed all the recipes and made many useful suggestions.

A sincere thank you must also go to the staff of the Mt. Prospect (Ill.) Public Library who were particularly helpful during the course of this project.

All of the recipes in this book were developed in my kitchen and critically taste-tested by my family and by the Rechners. While I've been making sausage, Bernie has been researching and writing the other parts of this volume. Her support and collaboration have made this book possible.

Bertie Mayone Selinger

A project of this nature is never a solitary undertaking—behind the printed page are dozens of people who contributed their time, interest, and knowledge so that the idea would become a reality.

I am particularly grateful to Bertie Selinger who shares her friendship and expertise. Without Bertie there would be no book.

Very special thanks must go to my husband Ed for his support and encouragement, for the hours of artistic talent he contributed, for his perceptive culinary critiques, and for his analysis of the technical parts of the manuscript.

Our children, Carolyn, Kevin, and John, also deserve very special thanks for their sausage critiques, and their comments and suggestions which brought so much to the project. Thanks too to John for assembling smokers and to John and Kevin who helped convert the whiskey barrel into our homemade smoker—contributions which added much to the book, to our menus, and to our summer activities.

I am grateful to my mother-in-law Marie Kramer Rechner, and to my sister-in-law Therese Sullivan Rechner, both of whom loaned us manual meat grinders for experimentation.

Diane and Mario Bartelotti graciously shared their insight and experience about smoking sausage. I appreciate their helpfulness.

From the food service industry came consistent and congenial aid. I deeply appreciate the help of Mary E. Galloway, Agricultural Marketing Services, United States Department of Agriculture, Chicago; Fran Altman, National Hot Dog and Sausage Council, Chicago; Tom McDermott, National Livestock and Meat Board, Chicago; Lucille Lampman, International Natural Sausage Casings Council, Chicago; Kathy Mittelmeier, Griffith Laboratories U.S.A., Alsip, Ill.; A. Judson Burdick, Union Carbide, Bedford Park, Ill.; Carolyn Lewis, National Pork Producers Council, Des Moines, Iowa; Ms. Ferris, Department of Health, Education and Welfare, Public Health Service, Food and Drug Administration, Chicago; Jane Anderson, American Meat Institute, Arlington, Va.; Marshall Neale, American Spice Trade

Association, New York City; Linda Posati, United States Department of Agriculture, Washington, D.C.; and Art Bruesewitz, Sheboygan Sausage Co., Sheboygan, Wisc.

Thanks for assistance must also go to resource people at the Mt. Prospect (Ill.) Library; at Chicago Cutlery, Minneapolis; Wusthof-Trident, Inc., Boston; Smoker Products, Mabank, Texas; Bosman Industries, Shreveport, La.; University of Illinois Extension Service, Consumer Call-In, Chicago; Weber-Stephen Products, Co., Arlington Heights, Ill.; Oregon State University Extension Office, Corvallis, Ore.; Maid of Scandinavia, Minneapolis; General Mills, Inc., Minneapolis.

Not to be forgotten are the members of the cheering section—relatives, and personal, business, and professional friends whose interest and encouragement make me eternally grateful. To each of you, my thanks.

Bernadine Sellers Rechner

Index